Welcome to Zimmerton

facebook.com/RainyDayWriters

Welcome to Zimmerton

Quirky Characters and Really Good Pie

by The Rainy Day Writers

facebook.com/RainyDayWriters

Welcome to Zimmerton
Print Edition

Welcome to Zimmerton Copyright 2023, Kindle Direct Publishing. Printed and bound in the United States of America. All rights reserved. No part of this book may be used or reproduced in any manner whatsoever—except by a reviewer who may quote brief passages in a review—without written permission from the publisher.

Dedication

Bob Ley

BOB LEY IS A NAME familiar to citizens of Cambridge. When we think of Bob, we think of a man who has spent most of his life trying to make Cambridge a better place to live and work.

Bob joined the Rainy Day Writers in 2013 and participated in writing ten of their books. As with any group, changes in membership occurred, and Bob stepped up serving as president for several years. A true leader, Bob guided RDW as we sharpened our writing skills and collaborated in the publication of family friendly reading material.

Arriving in Cambridge, Bob opened Robert's Men's Shop in 1963. He ran it successfully for 42 years. After closing the store, he accepted the nomination to be the Safety/Service Director for the city of Cambridge. Six years later, he retired from that post.

Retirement didn't mean a life of leisure for Bob and his wife Sue. When they were visiting Oglebay Park's Festival of Lights, it occurred to them that something similar might be an answer to their quest to bring visitors into Cambridge and revitalize the downtown area. With their ideas as guideposts and the help of many volunteers, The Dickens Victorian Village Project became a reality.

Bob's creativity isn't limited to writing. He is a talented painter producing lovely landscapes. He has also written his own series of novels about the lives of classmates who emerged from high school and took very different paths as adults. His *Class of '59* series can be purchased on Amazon.

To be closer to his children and grandchildren, Bob relocated to Newark, Ohio. RDW members appreciated Bob's tenacity in traveling back to Cambridge for meetings and work sessions, but the miles took their toll, and Bob resigned in January of 2023. Before bowing out of our literary group, he left us with the idea for our 2023 book, *Welcome to Zimmerton*. John Zimmer, founder of the town named for him, is Bob's brainchild.

It is with affection and gratitude that Rainy Day Writers dedicate this volume of stories to our friend Bob Ley.

Table of Contents

Dedication	v
Acknowledgements	ix
Author Biographies	x
Foreword – Welcome to Zimmerton	xiii
Cast of Characters	xiv
My Hometown by Betsy Taylor	1
Coming to Zimmerton by Judy Simcox	4
Thoroughly Modern Zoe by Judy Simcox	8
All-American Girls by Judy Simcox	14
Accretion by Judy Simcox	21
The Legend of Hoop by Mark Cooper	27
Front Porch Sittin' by Betsy Taylor	31
The Farmer Boys by Martha F. Jamail	37
Faith and Hope by Claire Cameron	40
Bossy and Her Hill by Mark Cooper	49
Gypsy Wagon Comes to Town by Beverly Wencek Kerr	55
Miracle on Goodyear Road by Samuel D. Besket	63
Zimmerton Mercantile by Claire Cameron	67
Grandpa's Favorite Sweet Treat by Beverly Wencek Kerr	75

Rose by Samuel D. Besket	81
Second Time Around by Samuel D. Besket	87
Harpo the Hobo by Claire Cameron	93
A to Z – Angelico to Zimmerton by Martha F. Jamail	96
The Prince and the Refrigerator by Mark Cooper	100
Shenanigans by Claire Cameron	103
Bonnie's Gypsy Spirit Lives On by Beverly Wencek Kerr	110
Stuff That Happens at Stan's Station by Mark Cooper	117
Discovering Zimmerton for Christmas by Mark Cooper	121
Family by Betsy Taylor	128
Neighbors by Betsy Taylor	137
Sally Stops at Stan's Station by Mark Cooper	145
Happy 100th Birthday by Beverly Wencek Kerr	149
The Feud by Samuel D. Besket	154
Zimmerton Zeke, the Worst Weather-Predicting Groundhog Ever by Rick Booth	160

Acknowledgements

RAINY DAY WRITERS WISH TO thank our faithful readers for following us as we produce our annual publications. We're grateful for your feedback and your support. Comments about our Got-A-Minute stories published on yourradioplace.com and our monthly articles in Crossroads Magazine fuel our enthusiasm to continue writing interesting, family friendly stories for your enjoyment.

While we couldn't have produced our work without you in mind, we must also recognize and thank these generous friends who support us in so many ways. You are encouraged to patronize these fine organizations.

- AVC Communications
- Crossroads Library
- Crossroads Magazine
- Cambridge News
- Country Bits
- Dickens Welcome Center
- Ellie's Cottage
- Guernsey County History Museum
- Modern Movements
- Mosser Glass
- Mr. Lee's Restaurant
- Nothing But Chocolate
- The Museum Association of East Muskingum
- The Station on 22
- The Townehouse Gifts and Interiors

Author Biographies

Betsy Taylor loves visiting Zimmerton, especially in the summer when townsfolk and visitors fill the town square. Her friends Richard and Cleo Babic often meet her at Martha's Place for lunch and pie. The best visits include a trip to the Stylette and a stop at her cousin Zeb's farm.

Beverly Wencek Kerr enjoys travelng anywhere any time. Many call her Gypsy Bev. She would liked to grow up in Zimmerton next to Bonnie Byers's farm to hear the stories of the gypsies who camped there. Like Bonnie, Bev always dreamed of traveling in all fifty states. Dreams do come true.

Bob Ley, a life-long entrepreneur who successfully transitioned to public service, shows his creative side when he writes and paints. Bob knows Zimmerton well. He and John Zimmer, the town's founder, have much in common. They could have met at Martha's Place on any day for lunch, a cup of coffee, and a discussion about local affairs.

Claire Cameron, inspired by childhood memories of tending her granddad's country store, tells the story of Gracie Mae and Adam Carlisle who operate Zimmerton Mercantile. Busy with her own family, Claire doesn't visit Zimmerton often but has fond memories of its rustic charm.

Harriette McBride Orr is a life-long Guernsey County resident where she is active in her community. She hasn't been able to visit Zimmerton this year. But RDW wish to acknowledge her unfailing advice, encouragement and support for our endeavor.

Judy Simcox has lived in seven states and always in small towns, preferring them to cities, or in the country where it's too quiet. A town like Zimmerton is like a Mr. Rogers community – deliberately paced and optimistic, where everybody knows everybody.

Mark Cooper lives on a farm and works at a gas station. If you look for him in Zimmerton, you might find him enjoying coffee at Stan's Station or feasting on pie from Martha's. But you won't see him driving down Bossy's Hill, at least not in winter.

Martha Jamail was born in Clarksdale, a small town in Mississippi. When she married, she moved to Cambridge, Ohio. Clarksdale and Cambridge are alive with the friendly atmosphere of Zimmerton. As a Rainy Day Writer, Martha is able to use her artistic and storytelling abilities to help bring Zimmerton and its characters to life.

Rick Booth used to program video games, design digital video software, and work for Sesame Street on the East Coast before returning to Cambridge, his hometown, where he researches and writes on local history. He suspects that the groundhog who lives under his barn is a cousin of Zimmerton Zeke.

Sam Besket, a lifelong resident of Guernsey County, was born into a family of coal miners. His father and grandfather worked at Zimmerton Coal Mine before moving to Guernsey County when the mine closed. An avid reader, Sam and his wife Carolyn reside in Byesville, Ohio.

Welcome to Zimmerton

ZIMMERTON, A SMALL OHIO TOWN much like yours, lies in the eastern part of the state where natural resources have given birth to industries that have enriched the lives of its citizens. Coal, oil, natural gas, lush forests, rich soil for farming, and abundant clay deposits have allowed Ohioans to put food on their tables and provide good futures for their children.

Ohio has a strong, rich history flush with stories that hark from prehistoric times. But this visit to our town won't take you back that far. You'll have to look elsewhere for stories about dinosaurs that roamed the land and the prehistoric Native Americans who built the great mounds. Instead, we'll begin our tales with the town's namesake, John Zimmer.

To be sure, the town was named for Zimmer, but a settlement and a train stop already existed before he arrived and decided to make this small community his home. Young, enthusiastic, and visionary, Zimmer was a driving force in the evolution of a hamlet into a town.

While the railroad made Zimmerton a convenient place to stop and conduct business, amenities like shops, churches, and schools soon made it an attractive place to put down roots.

Between these pages, you'll encounter a host of characters who call Zimmerton home. Through their stories, you'll watch Zimmerton grow and flourish. You'll also meet some folks who only pass through town but leave a bit of themselves behind.

Come along with the Rainy Day Writers and become acquainted with townspeople whom you might (or might not) want to invite into your circle of friends.

Cast of Characters

Alicia Szabo – elementary teacher who found and old family recipe

Amelia Angelico – young lady who moves from Vermont to Zimmerton to study nursings

Annik Miskonnen – came to Zimmerton at age nine from Finland to work in her family's limestone quarry

Bob West – wounded war veteran

Bonnie Byers – child, then waitress with a gypsy spirit that led her on many adventures

Eli Zook – married Zoe Michaledes

Faith and Hope – Reverend Fitzgerald's strong-willed adopted twins

Frank Byers – life-long Zimmerton for 100 years, lived on the family farm

Georgina Berry – newspaper cub reporter just starting to understand Zimmerton

Gracie Mae – precocious granddaughter of Adam Carlisle, Owner of Zimmerton Mercantile

Harpo – juice-harp playing hobo passing through Zimmerton

Hoop – a character, a legend, and a voice!

Jason and Sue Schmidt – Owners of Zimmerton Heating and Cooling

Jim Lindsay – oldest son who helps his father work on their farm in Zimmerton

Jody – a city gal who discovers unexpected Christmas joy in a small town

Justin Von – retired auto parts manager

Lucious McAllister – Zimmerton mayor and shocked recipient of a flying strawberry pie

Marley Davis – young woman searching for her roots in Zimmerton

Miri – daughter of gypsies who gave Bonnie the spirit to travel

Monty Ables – the man Annik married

Pete and Petie Erickson – mischief passes down through generations

Pop Prichard – blacksmith turned auto-repairman

Richard and Cleo Babic – retired couple who uncovered a scheme to steal gold

Rick Duncan – businessman

Shirley Moore – retired meteorologist

Zedekiah – overly conscientious employee at Stan's Station

Zoe Michaledes – came to Zimmerton at age nine from Greece with her family to work in their Greek restaurant

Zeb Hosfelt – local farmer who trusts his rodent and perspicacious parrot

My Hometown
Betsy Taylor

I LOVE MY HOMETOWN. Like most of us in the Zimmer Family, I was born here. The grandson of John Zimmer, I was christened John Zimmer III, but everyone called me Three. Unlike Grandpa, I was always content to remain right here. Even a short hiatus in college and a look at the outside world wasn't enough of a temptation to lure me permanently from Zimmerton.

While I understood Grandpa's urge to strike out on his own, I was destined for a different path. My goal to strengthen and preserve our town came with the family's entrepreneurial spirit. A merchant at heart, I knew the town would only grow if there were businesses to employ our citizens.

During the 1920s, coal mining became a huge business and outsiders flocked to Zimmerton. Some of those folks brought families, and, even when the coal played out, those folks stayed.

Like a lot of small towns, Zimmerton has had its ups and downs. During one of the good times, I was able to convince my dad to throw in with me and create an honest-to-goodness mercantile. Okay, it was a glorified general store with a fancy name, but it drew customers from the surrounding area and travelers as they passed through.

Over time, the mercantile grew to live up to its name. I'm proud to say, it provided jobs for scores of people, and put food on the table for many families.

Take a stroll with me as I walk through town. The showpiece is the town square. But look at that massive gazebo gleaming white in the sun. Our Community Preservation Society does a terrific job of tending to it and the carousel. The gazebo is the site of weddings and events. The carousel is run by a volunteer every Saturday during warm weather. And picnickers are welcome to spread a blanket and a meal on the lawn anytime.

Some of the businesses around the square have been here for generations. Martha's Place is an example. Her great grandmother opened the restaurant in 1920, and it was an instant success. Martha uses the same recipe for her famous strawberry pie, and she guards it like the treasure it is.

Look. There's Karl's Shoes. That store has supported the family for four generations while making sure Zimmertonians were well shod.

Over there is the grade school. Well, they call it Zimmerton Elementary now. I notice that the kids still line up at recess for a game of Red Rover.

The high school is nearby. Oh, there's Martha taking advantage of this grand weather to hold her art class outside. She has them sitting on the lawn drawing pictures of the John Zimmer statue. I swear, that woman is a marvel. She teaches art in the morning and heads to the restaurant in the afternoon to feed a passel of hungry diners.

Over, about a block, is Pop's Auto Repair. Pop was quite a character. He could fix just about anything. The town is lucky that his grandkids have expanded the business and kept it going.

Follow me around the corner and you'll see the telephone store. They call it a cell phone store now. I sure never thought the idea would catch on. But look at all the people on the street just staring at those little boxes.

This is where the fire station used to be. They had to move it to the edge of town when the trucks got to be so big and fast. The hospital had to move for the same reason. Just needed more space. Of course, those lots were gobbled up when the Daily Zimmertonian needed more room. Zimmerton is fortunate to maintain a daily newspaper when so many towns have seen an end to local news in print.

Right beside the newspaper office is the First Baptist Church, one of the first churches established here. Reverend Fitzgerald takes good care of his flock. Stop in on any Sunday morning and you'll receive a warm welcome.

Other towns may boast of a supermarket, but we still have our Corner Grocery Store. Local farmers have a place to sell their produce and our townsfolk can buy fresh-from-the-farm food. This is Zimmerton Heating and Cooling. I can promise you Jason Schmidt responds whenever he's needed. Why, several winters past, the man struck out in one of our worst blizzards to restore power to a good portion of our residents.

The Stylette is another small business that's still here. We're proud that ladies can buy quality clothing without the bother of traipsing off to the big city. A nice lady named Shirley Bates owns it now.

Finally, we've come to the mercantile. Over time, it's been sold to Adam Carlisle. After all these years, I'm still attached to this place. From the front window I can look out and watch folks come and go through our thriving town.

Yes, indeed. I love my hometown today just as much as I did when I was alive.

Coming to Zimmerton
Judy Simcox

ANNIK AND ZOE MET ON the first day of fourth grade at Zimmerton Grade School. Annik was almost albino-like in her paleness, her hair nearly white. Zoe was olive-skinned with rosy cheeks, her hair black as a raven's wing. They were both nine years old with long braids and quaint modes of dress. The girls sat side by side alphabetically because Annik's last name was Miskonnen and Zoe's was Michaledes.

Annik's family had come to Zimmerton in June from Finland via Nova Scotia at the invitation of her father's uncle. Her father was to work in the family's stone cutting business. Zoe's family had come in July so that her parents could work at the Aegean, the Greek restaurant her grandfather had started. Neither spoke English past a few words like "yes", "no", "please", "thank you", "mama", and "home."

Mrs. Cook, the principal of Zimmerton Grade School, had to do some research and consult experts at the state level to discover the recommended path for her sudden influx of immigrants needing to learn English. She collected a file along with instructions for the task. Then she decided to tackle the assignment herself. She missed the days of classroom teaching, and figured she'd have time for her administrative duties and this, too. Two days later, she had a schedule, a time frame, and a plan. She welcomed the two girls into the nook she'd prepared behind her office.

"Hello," she said softly to their deer-in-the-headlights faces. "I'm Mrs. Cook." She pointed to her own chest. "You are Annik?" Annik flushed nervously as she smiled. "Yes?" Mrs.

Cook asked pointing to the child.

"Yes," Annik replied.

Zoe eagerly awaited her introduction. Mrs. Cook pointed to her but did not speak. She did raise her eyebrows in question.

"Yes!" Zoe exclaimed. "Zoe," she announced pointing to herself. "Annik," she said pointing to her companion, and pointing to her teacher, she said, "Mrs. Cook." Everybody smiled.

For an hour every day while their classmates waded into the thickets of arithmetic and geography, the three assembled in the little space and learned English along with a smattering of sign language of their own invention. Pointing to oneself meant "I", and to someone else meant "you." Thumbs up meant "like", and, eventually, a hand on the heart meant "love."

They learned quickly and steadily. By the Christmas holiday, they were ready to return to their classroom. Still, they came to her with questions about the names of things and the meaning of puzzling phrases. They leaned on each other, too. Both could read, but Zoe was learning a new alphabet. Annik helped her slog along.

They walked most of the way home together each afternoon, and part way back to school in the mornings. The two friends memorized their route by noting the landmarks like the Mobil station with the flying horse sign. "Pegasus!" Zoe observed. Annik puzzled over that. The word that sprang to her mind was "hevonen", Finnish for "horse."

Annik took paper and pencil and sketched a clear picture of the sign, intending to ask Mrs. Cook. Eyes wide, Zoe exclaimed over the drawing. "I like Pegasus," she exclaimed.

Annik made sketches of the mailbox where they turned left and the stone house with the turret where they parted ways. The next day, she eagerly produced the sketches which surprised and delighted Mrs. Cook who had come to love her little learners.

"Pegasus," Zoe stated firmly.

"Pegasus is . . . Mrs. Cook replied slowly, "a flying horse."

"Horse." Each girl repeated the word.

With an inquiring expression, Annik made a clicking sound and jostled in her seat as though riding. "Horse?"

"Yes," Mrs. Cook replied smiling. The girls looked at each other.

"I like horse," Annik said. Zoe nodded her agreement.

"Pegasus is a flying horse," Mrs. Cook continued flapping her hands by her shoulders like little wings.

"No flying horses. Not real," Annik huffed, sketching a bird in flight.

"Yes, birds fly," Mrs. Cook agreed.

"Birds fly," the girls repeated in unison.

"Pegasus is a myth." This was too far into the deep end. "Pretend," Mrs. Cook continued.

"Pretend," they repeated.

Annik reached tentatively for Mrs. Cook's ubiquitous red pencil. When she was allowed to grasp it, she colored the flying horse and looked questioningly at her teacher.

"Red," said Mrs. Cook.

Annik held up the pencil. "Red," she repeated. Looking around, she settled on Zoe's hair ribbon. Touching it, she announced, "red."

Annik displayed her sock. "Blue," said Mrs. Cook.

Again, they explored and held up a book with a picture of the sea on the cover. Pointing at the water, they repeated, "Blue." The teacher nodded. A leafy plant in the window yielded the word "green", a number two pencil was pronounced "yellow", and the table where they sat, "brown."

"Colors," Mrs. Cook Said. "All these are colors."

"Colors," the two repeated dutifully. With Anik's sketches, Zoe's ideas, and Mrs. Cook's patience, they learned a lot that autumn.

As December approached, Annik and Zoe were perplexed

listening to their classmates talk about how they celebrated Christmas, American-style. Annik connected it to the Lutheran religious holiday her family observed, but, by comparison, the American observance was gaudy and enticing. Zoe also had to ponder the contrast of the American holiday with her background. Her Greek Orthodox family observed the festivities accompanying Jesus's birth on January 6th.

They agreed to mark both dates with their own celebrations. Annik taught Zoe to make traditional straw stars after they had gleaned the shiniest, most golden straw they could find in the neighboring farmer's field. "Tahti," she called them. "Asteri," Zoe said. "Asteri in the night sky."

Zoe brought a little bag of kouribiades to Annik's house after helping her mother and grandmother make many dozens of them. Annik and her mother each took one to sample. Annik's toddler brother Aimo took one in each hand. When he finished gobbling them down, he looked like an old man with a long white beard made of powdered sugar. Annik almost drooled while eating hers. They were luscious. But, over time, her favorite Michaledes baked treat was baklava.

Thoroughly Modern Zoe

Judy Simcox

ANNIK AND ZOE MET TO walk to Zimmerton High School on the first day of ninth grade. Each had spent a busy summer with little time to socialize. Annik worked in the office of her family's stone works. She helped with bookkeeping, advertising, billing, and dealing with customers since she could speak English. By this time, she, her younger brother Aimo, and an older cousin all spoke English fluently. Her parents trailed the youngsters in the use of the language.

Zoe spent the summer inadvertently creating a bake shop adjacent to her grandparents' restaurant, the Aegean. She had become such an enthusiastic, just-plain-good baker of Greek cookies and sweets that she began to explore other baking styles –Italian, Spanish, Turkish, and even Egyptian. A generous cookie became a delicious breakfast for students on the run, working men, and those just goin' fishin'.

The girls had both become expert seamstresses, making their own clothes, and helping others. Their outfits had changed from dirndls and blouses, lavishly embroidered to reflect their ethnic heritage. They now wore sparsely trimmed clothing with rows of buttons and self-belts. They still wore their hair in long braids raised off their backs in a knot at the crown or pulled back and hanging down. However, they looked longingly at their classmates, at women in public, and even women at church, and yearned to bob their hair.

Zoe acquired a women's magazine left in the Aegean Restaurant. The girls sat outside one day examining a single photograph.

"See how her hair is cut bluntly on each side but on a slant, shorter at the nape and a little longer at her jaw. It is parted in the middle like we do our braids, and it's lopped off easy as pie," Zoe mused, her fingers traveling over the picture.

"It looks like Mary Jane Lowery," Annik remarked naming a classmate whose family indulged her in many ways. "I bet she spends some money on her hair cuts."

"But it looks easy," Zoe insisted. "Doesn't your mother cut your brothers' hair?"

"And my dad's and my cousin's."

"So, she has scissors for cutting hair. My mom has scissors for nothing but fabric. And my dad's scissors can only cut paper and twine. You must have special scissors for cutting hair."

"Yes, the scissors Mama uses have little round finger holes, not like sewing scissors at all."

"We need to get hold of them."

"And we need to make sure they're as sharp as can be."

"Yes. And we need to braid our hair close and tight so it's all together in a handful. We must part it very carefully and have ribbons on hand to tie up the ends. We also need boxes to put them in to keep."

"Why do we need to keep them?"

"To make hairpieces. My grandmother has a braided bun she pins on the back of her head. It looks funny because it's a different color from her hair now."

"You're sure you want to do this?" Annik asked in a whisper.

"Yes, I'm sure," Zoe answered decisively. "Our hair will be a lighter load and a-la-mode."

Within a week, Annik had the scissors that she had given a turn on the sharpening wheel in her father's shop. She also brought a wooden cigar box. Zoe brought a box, a handful of ribbons, and a growing knot in her stomach. She had learned that the braided bun her grandmother pinned behind her head was really her great-grandmother's hair cut off when the old woman died. Her grandmother's hair had never been cut, only thinned by age and the travails of her life.

The girls sat under an isolated tree on a warm autumn afternoon and braided each other's hair. They meticulously parted and combed close to their hairlines behind their ears. Next, they tied each braid at the bottom and the top. They trimmed off the ends of the hair to help them get a feel for the scissors. If they didn't hold the braid tight, the scissors would slip. Preparations complete, the girls sat in silence for half an hour. Finally, Zoe proffered the scissors to her trusted sister-friend and said, "You go first."

Annik grasped Zoe's thick black braid. She adjusted her grip to be firm an inch or two from the scalp and cut finding she had to saw through the rope of hair. The two-foot braid came away and the remaining hair sprang back in a surprising mass of bouncing waves. The weight of Zoe's hair had hidden its natural curl. Neither spoke. Zoe placed the braid into her box. "Okay," she said. "Finish it. Cut the other braid."

Annik repeated the process. Zoe put her hands on her head and began to breathe rapidly. They discovered they had come without a mirror. "How does it look?" she whispered anxiously.

"Like magic," Annik said. "It's curled all over. Just beautiful."

Zoe sat staring at the braids in the box. Glancing up, she saw Annik waiting for her turn. Taking the scissors, she cut off her friend's flaxen, straight braids. The bob lay symmetrically close to Annik's head. The style would become known as the Dutch Boy bob. In silence they gathered up their boxes, tied each shut with an extra ribbon, assembled their other possession, and headed home.

Shy with her new look, Annik lay low all evening out of sight in the workshop. She begged off dinner and went to her room. When darkness came, she looked out the window at the huge maple tree. In the streetlight's glow she saw a crumpled shape pressed against the trunk. It stirred and made a mournful sound. The shape was Zoe!

Annik raced down the back stairs, out the door, and circled around the house unseen.

Crouching at the base of the tree, Zoe held her hands over her ears. Blood ran down the side of her face. She looked wordlessly up at Annik who dropped beside her enveloping her in her arms. "I didn't know where else to go," Zoe choked.

"You came to the right place," Annik answered.

The girls stood up and tried to sneak back upstairs. But Annik's mother, Enni, who had brought a little food to her room, opened the door, and called her name.

Zoe and Annik emerged into the hallway, lit by a single bulb. Annik's tall, slim mother stared from one girl to the other. "My dear," she said reaching out to Zoe, "you're bleeding."

Zoe sat on Annik's bed as a pitcher of water was poured into a large bowl. Annik's mother gently applied a moist cloth to Zoe's red skin. Where the hair was shorn, she found two cuts on Zoe's scalp.

"What did you girls do to your hair?" cried Annik's mother.

"We bobbed our hair, Mama, but I didn't do that! We wanted to look like American girls." She hugged Zoe and waited.

Enni collected herself while she wrung out the cloth and applied it further to Zoe's head. Zoe began to cry.

"Am I hurting you?" Enni asked.

"No," Zoe hiccupped. "I wish my family could have accepted it like you."

"Well, you can't put back what's cut off," Enni said. "How did your family react?"

"My mother was upset, disappointed, I think." My grandmother came running out waving the kitchen shears and shrieking, "Do you want to look like a boy? Then you'll look like a boy!" She grabbed my hair and hacked off a couple of pieces, cutting my head and nearly stabbing me in the face. My mother pulled her back. I got away and ran. Can I come and live with you?"

"Well, you can stay here tonight and stay in tomorrow, if you want to. We'll have a look at your hair in the morning and talk to your mother when she comes around."

"You think she'll come looking for me?"

"Of course, she will," promised Enni softly as she closed the door.

The next day, Zoe's mother, Sofia, did indeed come around bearing a box of baklava. By that time, Enni, who had great skill as a barber, had trimmed Zoe's boisterous curls into a shapely cap that hardly revealed the shorn patch. She had also trimmed and evened out Annik's bob.

"Although I worried, I knew Zoe would come here," said Sofia. "Please try to understand. My mother has taken the move to America very badly. Neither she nor any of her ancestors, except for men who were drafted, had ever left our village. She grew up there, raised four children there, and looked to die there, until we had to move. I couldn't leave her alone, but she hates it here. Always, she is sad and angry. To her, Zoe's long hair represented the wisdom of the old ways. Zoe has turned things upside down all along. Her schooling, working out in public, her mode of dress, all of it. I am sorry...helpless...torn between..."

Sofia clutched the hand that Enni held out. "Thank you for sheltering her!" she blurted.

"Of course. She can stay here until things sort out, if that would help. Maybe, somehow, get some separation from her grandmother."

"I don't know but things will have to settle down. May I see Zoe?"

"Yes. Any time you need to. Girls," she called. The two descended the last three or four steps from where they had perched eavesdropping.

"I'm sorry, Mama, for disappointing you," Zoe cried.

"You never disappoint me, Moro Mou," her mother said. "You are becoming an American woman." She held Zoe by her shoulders. "And your curls are beautiful."

All-American Girls

Judy Simcox

ZOE'S FATHER INSTALLED A SMALL SPACE with a desk and a cot behind the extension where they'd put the bake shop. Here Zoe could achieve separation from her grandmother and from the restaurant.

And Annik was invited to learn to play basketball. After only a short time, she discovered that she loved it. Most of her teammates were boys. As she acquired new skills, she generally out-paced, out-scored, and out-maneuvered them. Although they usually traded good-natured sass, the trash-talk sometimes became heated. Soon, with the boys, she was just one of the boys, but from the girls and some teachers, she earned vague disapproval.

Though she was still her best friend, Zoe had other girl-friends, too. They gathered in art class and in girls' gym class where they played volleyball and danced with hoops in small groups. Annik sometimes heard a few of those girls whispering and, when she came near, they turned away. As Annik matured, some of the boys turned away, too. Most of them were still cordial but often practice was just ending when she took the court. Annik faced the fact that she had become neither fish nor fowl.

By her 16th birthday, Annik had given up basketball and was firmly in the "girl" category.

By this time Zoe was becoming well-known for her after school baking and money-making. The small extension her father had installed beside the Aegean Restaurant had become Zoe's bake shop. She continued to live there in an uneasy truce with her grandmother who was as flinty as ever and becoming increasingly odd. In her mind, she lived largely in the past in Greece. Zoe and her mother grew closer. Sophia was relieved and grateful for the added income from Zoe's bakery. Her father and brothers became more congenial consuming about 20% of her product.

When the friends turned 17, war intruded in Zimmerton. The air was filled with roiling, disturbed spirits. First came astonishment as if people were startled from sleep by some great noise. Then came anger followed by a sudden linking of arms proclaiming unity. Words like "us", "we", "Americans" were heralded in a surge of genuine, tear-inducing love of country. Young men, some from the basketball team, and Eino, Annik's cousin lined up to enlist in the army. Some were inducted and some, like Eino, were classified as 4F and were rejected.

By the time Zoe and Annik graduated, four of their friends had been drafted as soon as they'd turned 18. Annik was close with one basketball boy, Tommy Nolan. As he had developed into a varsity basketball star, he continued practicing with her while he honed his shooting skills and basked in her admiration. Suddenly he was drafted. Feeling pulled from his world, he reached for Annik. Without Zimmeron High and basketball, he felt lost, confused, and anxious. Tommy's dad was often gone working on the railroad and his mother was absorbed caring for her five younger children. Annik was his touchstone.

When he went to the capitol to board a train for boot camp, Annik went with him. Before he had to leave, on a whim, they found City Hall. They raced from office to office but couldn't pull together a way to get married. Instead, Tommy hurried Annik to a jeweler and bought her a modest diamond. "The little diamond that could," they called it. He begged her to marry him when he got leave after basic training. She already had doubts but consented. Then he was gone.

BACK IN ZIMMERTON, Annik showed the ring to Zoe first.

"Tommy Nolan?" Zoe asked. Annik nodded solemnly.

"I'll be Nikky Nolan," she quipped. "He calls me Nick."

Zoe pulled a face. "I didn't even realize you were sweet on him, or anyone."

Annik hesitated. "Neither did I," she said. "How about you? Are you sweet?"

Zoe thought a moment. "Not really. The guy I like to talk to, to work with is Eli."

"The Amish man? He's so old."

"He's not Amish anymore," Zoe replied. "He's 27 and he knows his way around a kitchen. Also, he has six beehives. Good for the baklava."

"If you get married," Annik teased, "you'll be Zoe Zook." They both laughed.

Eli was indeed a part of Zoe's life now. And Annik could tell there was a spark.

Annik settled into life at the quarry that had turned almost exclusively to the production of crushed limestone. She created a system to handle the tidal wave of demand for #3 gravel needed to build roads and airfields. Her parents knew about her engagement and often spoke about it with her.

She received letters from Tommy that were full of chatter about the changes in his life, and his homesickness. He told Annik how much he missed her, but she could see that there was no evidence of ardent longing.

Annik wrote back in the same vein. Searching her heart for some focus of feeling, she found only fondness and hope for good outcomes. She shed tears over her failing. She did not visit his parents.

And then he was gone.

On some grueling training exercise, he fell down a stone escarpment and died. She shed many tears then and put the diamond in a drawer. Along with many of his schoolmates, including Zoe, she attended his funeral service. There she saw his parents with their five younger hopes and dreams. Mrs. Nikky Nolan would never be.

Two years later, however, Zoe Zook came to be. Zoe and Eli married in a quiet, nearly secret ceremony that the grim-jawed grandmother knew nothing about. In due time, Zoe delivered twin girls whom she named Sofia for her mother and Sarah for Eli's. There were no more children.

Annik gave Zoe an outdoor clay oven for a wedding gift. She got the idea while watching Zoe take flatbread out of a coal-fired metal stove with a metal spatula.

"I have an idea for a great art project made by the Miskonnen Brothers' Limestone Quarry," she told herself. Almost everything she needed was at hand – rock of all sizes, sand, and cranes and trucks to move it all. She picked a flat spot near a windowless wall of the bakery and piled her materials on ground already tamped from past piling and parking.

Zoe didn't notice anything going on until the oven was almost finished, but Eli did.

"What goes here?" he inquired in accented English.

Annik stood for a breath and said, "I'm making a clay oven for Zoe."

"Which she doesn't know?" His brows rose into his straw-colored hair.

"It's a gift for your wedding."

"Ah," he murmured cracking his knuckles. "I can help?" he asked.

"Well. Okay. I'm just about finished with the foundation."

Eli walked around it, pushing at places, eyeing the corners, and digging at hollows with his fingers. "Not solid enough," he announced. "Needs more sand."

"I have lots of sand," she said. "Tons!" She pointed to a heap at the back of the lot.

Eli picked up a shovel and motioned her away. "I will get it in order."

Feeling dismissed, she returned to the quarry. "I could get it in order," she grumbled.

Of one thing she was uncertain – how to construct the clay dome. As she pondered her problem, a trucker who appeared to want to ingratiate himself with her darkened the door. Monty Ables had heard the same rumors she had. A huge national highway system was planned. Gravel would be in great demand as would trucks to haul it. That was the reason the quarry was switching almost exclusively to crushed limestone. Monty Ables was angling to become their principal hauler.

"Howzit goin', Ms. Miskonnen?" he asked.

"Annik is fine, Mr. Ables."

"Then Monty is fine, too, Annik. Heard any news through the grapevine?"

"Not since we spoke on Tuesday. I have a question though. I want to build an outdoor oven for my friend Zoe at the Aegean, and I don't know if the right kind of clay can be had around here."

"Well, not right in your backyard, but pretty close. I know where I can get you a truckload in Waterston that would be good for your purpose."

A smile lit Annik's face. "That would be great, Monty. Really great! What quantity? A couple of barrels or bags, or what?"

"It comes in a pile. You'll need a way to loosen it up. Don't worry about the cost. I can have it here on Saturday."

"No, I can't let you . . ." she objected.

"It's no problem," he laughed. "Call it a bribe." He took a handful of peppermints out of her jar and waved on the way out.

Annik hurried back to the job site where Eli had practically rebuilt the platform that was now solid as a rock. He stood admiring his work. He saw her approach and said, "You have to make a mound of sand in the middle to mold the clay around."

"You've done this before?" she asked. He nodded and she breathed easier. They managed to mold the mound that day covering it with cloth and an old sisal rug. After gathering what they thought they'd need to make the clay malleable, they quit for the day.

On Saturday morning, the clay arrived – a large mound in the bed of Monty's pickup truck. The stuff looked like cornmeal mush. Monty came dressed to pitch in. Together they loosened, pounded, manipulated, and applied the clay to the sand mound, a pancake-like piece at a time. When they finished, the clay on the mound was six inches thick.

Eli cut an arched opening on one side while Monty eyed him and Annik, his brow furrowed.

"This is for a wedding present. So far, it's a surprise only for the bride. Eli is the groom."

Monty relaxed.

Rather than paving the sides they studded the clay with limestone the size of a fist. The men laid plans to build a roof over the structure that could be open to the sun then closed to the rain. Zoe never peeked while they were working, although Annik suspected she was aware of the conspiracy. Annik's grandfather came to view the finished product. He had observed this kind of oven built in his homeland.

The dome dried, was sealed, and surrounded by a patio of pavers.

When the oven was revealed, Zoe might not have been surprised at the gift but her astonishment at its sophistication was real. She and her mother made flatbread wheels two feet across. The flatbread was popular with customers and brought new attention to the Aegean.

As an older woman, Annik also married an older man. She had become the manager of the quarry's production of #3 gravel to meet the ever-growing demand of road builders. She dealt with many trucking companies, but her relationship with Monty Ables strengthened. He handled more of her transportation needs and expanded his fleet. They grew prosperous in their partnership and married just before Annik's 40th birthday.

She laughed with Zoe. "So, you're Zoe Zook and I'm Annik Ables. We're All-American now from A to Z."

Accretion
Judy Simcox

ANNIK AND ZOE MOVED THROUGH TIME in the tranquil, small town of Zimmerton as the world changed around them. Zoe continued to bake flawless products that customers lined up to buy. Her husband, Eli Zook, and his brothers built an addition to the one her father constructed behind the bakery. He continued to act as her sous chef cherishing her and their twin girls. The twins, calling themselves Sophie and Sally, were the spark plugs of the family, their school, and their church. They sang together in lyric harmony, even composing songs and playing the flute and piano. They had a clutch of cousins. The family of kids wheeled around the place like a flock of birds. Their primary pastime was baseball.

Annik's family business, the limestone quarry, slowed down a bit as highway construction proceeded away from the area. Monty branched out into earth-moving services, delivering and spreading gravel, ditching, laying pipe and culverts, and removing trees and brush. Along the way he developed a skill with laying concrete.

Annik enjoyed keeping an eye on Zoe's girls, supporting their efforts as well as those of her and Zoe's nieces and nephews. She had no children, not even a dog, just a sun-loving old tabby cat. Then one day as she and Monty sat on the deck mulling over the weather forecast, the doorbell rang and changed their lives forever.

"Avon calling," Monty said sing-song, as Annik went to the door. When she opened it, a pleasant-looking twenty-something woman stood there with her arm around a boy who could have been ten or eleven. The child looked up, his face wet with tears, and Annik gasped.

"Monty," she called. "Would you come here, please?" She motioned the two inside and led them to sit on the couch. When Monty entered the room and looked at the child, Annik could see that his reaction was the same as hers.

"Are you Lamont George Ables?" the young woman asked as she opened a folder of documents.

"Yes," he replied.

"This young man is George Seeley," she said, "your son."

Abruptly Annik and Monty sat down, eyes wide in shock. She looked at him and he stared back blankly.

"Mr. Ables, George's mother was Barbara Seeley. Do you remember her?"

Monty looked from Annik to George to the woman gap-mouthed and mute.

The woman seemed to suddenly remember that she had not introduced herself. "I'm Darla Statts," she said producing a business card. "I'm from Child Protective Services."

"Was?" Annik spoke up. "Barbara Seeley was?"

The boy wiped his eyes and nose on his sleeve and gazed at Monty. Annik was struck by how much the two looked alike, right down to the worry lines between their brows.

Mrs. Statts fished another paper from the file and held it toward the couple. "This is George's birth certificate," she said. "His date of birth is October 18, 1957. This document names you, Mr. Ables, as his father. Barbara's name at the time was Jablonsky. She was a waitress at the Blue Moon Truck Stop in Toledo."

"Monty?" Annik urged as she touched his elbow.

"No," he stammered. "I don't remember." He looked at Annik. "That was before we were together. Trucking – it was like sailing the sea; I had a girl in every port. People would meet briefly and . . ."

Annik glimpsed the child as new tears fell.

Mrs. Statts flashed a grimace and said, "Well, that's for another time. George's family has come apart and he has no other relatives that we can locate. Legally, he belongs with you."

"What happened to Barbara?" Annik asked.

"She and Lewis Seeley were in a motorcycle accident," Mrs. Statts replied while pulling another paper from her folder. "This is a copy of her... certificate. The question is, can George stay here?"

Annik didn't hesitate. "Certainly." She rose and approached George.

"Mr. Ables?" the case worker queried.

Monty looked helplessly at Mrs. Statts.

She seemed to realize that her approach to the situation had lacked finesse. She motioned him aside out of hearing of young George. "I apologize for the way I've sprung all this on you and your wife. You should know that I never would have brought your son to you with no warning if the two of you hadn't been thoroughly investigated and cleared of all criminal history. Furthermore, you have both been determined to be people of good reputation. Please consider taking him in."

"I never not considered it. But..."

"It's a shock, I know."

"I doubt you do."

"George," called Mrs. Statts, "let's get your things."

George followed her to the door and returned alone with an over-stuffed backpack and a canvas tote. He stood stoop-shouldered at the door, small and dejected. Annika approached him slowly as he dropped his bags. She extended her hand, but he didn't take it. Instead, he searched he face as if her gaze held all the answers he needed.

"Are you hungry?" she asked. "Come and sit down." He sat when she did. "We're so sorry about your mother and Mr. Seeley. So hard for you, we know."

He looked from her to Monty who had come to sit beside him.

"I didn't . . . didn't . . ." Monty stuttered. He waved the papers Mrs. Statts had left. "I didn't . . ."

"She left my brother!" George blurted. "She didn't bring my brother! Are you going to keep me here?"

Annik looked at Monty.

"Yes, we are," he said.

"Then you have to get my brother!" the boy demanded firmly.

They looked at each other. "What brother? Where?" Annik looked at the social worker's card.

"He was with me at the home," George said.

Annik could do nothing else. She didn't even glance at her husband when she promised, "We'll find him, my dear." She inched closer. He leaned toward her and began to topple. She caught him and felt him shivering from head to foot.

They spent the next hour tempting him to eat some toast and warm milk, preparing the spare room for sleep, including a night light shaped like a puppy. He fell asleep as if he'd been clubbed, hugging an old teddy bear belonging to Annik's nephew.

The next morning, they paid a visit to Darla Statts' office. Monty sat with George in the lobby while Annik entered the arena. Surprised by the visit, Mrs. Statts appeared wary, in case the couple might want to return George.

She greeted Annik, "Let me apologize for yesterday. It was all so abrupt. I really didn't know what to do. My supervisor presented me with George and his paperwork and told me to take him to his father."

"George says he has a younger brother," was Annik's opening salvo.

"Yes, but he's not your husband's' child. He's only six. His name is Roger."

"Does he have family?"

"That's under investigation, but it looks like he doesn't. His dad was Lewis Seeley who seemed to have no close family."

"So, what happens to Roger?"

"He'll be put up for adoption."

"Put him with us. We'll take him," Annik said immediately.

Looking stunned, Darla sat. She appeared thoughtful. Then she picked up the phone and dialed. "This is Darla," she said into the receiver. "There's a woman in my office who needs to speak to you."

A moment later a small, round woman who looked like Mrs. Santa Claus entered. "I'm Lois Getty," she said introducing herself.

"This is Annik Ables, Lamont's wife," Darla said. "They've received George with great positivity, and they would like to take Roger, too."

"You want Roger, too? After having George for only one day? Do you have children of your own?"

"No. we came to it too late. What I have is a business, a home, and my husband's son who I will treat as my own and who yearns for his brother. He has no idea what's going on after having lost his parents and being shuffled around four weeks."

"Well," said Mrs. Getty decisively, "It just so happens that Roger is here today getting his picture taken. He could see George for a visit." With a spin of the phone's dial Mrs. Getty asked for Roger to be brought to Darla's office.

They moved to a small conference room where George sat close to Monty. Their resemblance was startling and brought a smile to Mrs. Getty's face.

"So, George, you miss your brother?" she asked.

"I don't know where he is," George lamented. "He's not with me and he had to stay with me."

"Do you think you'll be happy with Mr. and Mrs. Ables?"

"They came here to help me find Roger. I think they want us to be together."

"Is their house a nice place?"

"Oh, yes! I have a nice room that I can share with Roger. And their fridge is full."

A chuckle passed through the group. Suddenly the door opened to admit a woman holding the hand of a little boy in short pants. His hair was the color of marigolds.

"Georgie!" the child called out pulling his hand from his companion. He threw his arms around George's' waist. George put his arms around Roger's neck and clung weeping.

Mrs. Getty looked moved. "I think this tells the story," she said. "Roger, it appears that you want to stay with George, and, I think, Mr. and Mrs. Ables would be glad to take you both."

Together, Annik and Monty vowed that they'd like nothing better than to welcome the boys into their home.

"We'll start the paperwork right away, but a resolution may take months."

Annik and Monty nodded their understanding.

Mrs. Getty promised to send Roger's things to their home the next day and suggested that they go off for lunch.

"You have to send Clark, too," said Roger.

Annik sent a questioning look toward Mrs. Getty.

"Clark is their dog, a border collie. He's at the shelter."

"Clark?" said Monty. "George, Roger, Clark," he mused. "As in George Rogers Clark?"

"Mr. Seeley bestowed those names," Darla chuckled. "His given name was Meriwether Lewis Seeley."

So, Annik's family grew by two boys and a dog in one day. The boys and Clark were boisterous, and Monty and Eli had to fence in the backyard. They built a swing and sand box as well as a doghouse. More space was needed so the attic was repurposed for the youngsters. They soon had playmates. Two cousins, and the kid from down the street appeared at the back door and inquired, "Do you play baseball?"

The Legend of Hoop
Mark Cooper

HOOP WAS ONE OF ZIMMERTON'S LEGENDARY CITIZENS. He simply appeared one day. No one knew his real name or his actual age. Even though he looked ancient when he moved into the valley outside of town, "down in the holler" as old timers would say, he lived there for decades afterwards.

His thick beard reached almost to his waist. Long bushy hair fell down over his face and neck. Zimmerton's high flutin' society ladies sniffed through their upturned noses every time they saw him. "Never trust a man with hair covering his face," they'd say, "that means he's hiding something!" The sheriff frequently went by the path that led down into Hoop's holler. "I'm just keeping an eye on things," he'd say. But everyone knew he was really keeping an eye on Hoop.

Truth is, Hoop never bothered a soul. He didn't ask anything of anybody. Instead, he tried to help whenever he heard of someone in need. Many a time a sick citizen of Zimmerton would find a little bag of roots and herbs on their porch, along with a note baring Hoop's instructions for brewing a medicinal tea. On the note was scrawled, "This'll cure whatever ails ya." Surprisingly, those who dared to make and drink the concoction did seem to recover quickly.

Hoop's laugh was his most interesting characteristic. Starting as a low rumble deep in his throat, it would rise in pitch and volume until breaking free and filling the air with mirth. It was so loud that, if you were nearby, you'd think the ground was shaking. At the sound, alley cats hissed and ran away. Old coon dogs cut loose with mournful howls. The high flutin' society ladies trembled and pulled their shawls tighter around their shoulders. Men jeered, "Listen to that old fool holler'n, must be out of his mind." Young teen-aged boys smirked, "That crazy fool ought to be put away in the loony bin."

But Hoop lived by his own motto, "Laugh til it makes ya sick. Then laugh some more 'cause laughter is the best medicine." And Zimmerton's more thoughtful citizens noted that every time Hoop's laughter rang out, the town's babies and young kids giggled and laughed in pleasure and puppies wagged their tails.

One day, a couple of the old timers were enjoying coffee and pie at Martha's Place when one asked the other, "Have you seen Hoop for a while?"

"No, come to think of it, I haven't," his companion answered. They asked a few other people, and eventually the sheriff was notified that nobody had seen Hoop for some time. So, he and couple men went into the holler to check things out.

Hoop was simply gone. The menfolk searched high and low but found no evidence of him. His cabin was empty, no personal items were found, and there was no evidence it had been lived in for years. It was as if he'd never existed. People shook their heads over the mystery of Hoop. Some went as far as to say he'd maybe been a ghost, and they forbade their children from ever walking down towards the holler. The preacher's wife held fast he'd been an angel, sent to bring joy to those willing to receive it. That theory really made the high-flutin' ladies of Zimmerton snort in disapproval.

As time went by, the townspeople began to realize that regardless of who Hoop was, he'd left something of himself behind. Once in a rare while, a wild roaring sound with strangely pleasant undertones could be heard all the way from Hoop's valley to Zimmerton's town square.

The town's self-proclaimed weather expert insisted that the unusual sound resulted from a cold front combining just so with a hot front to create some sort of middle front that then rushed up from the holler.

But the old timers, those who really knew, nodded their heads wisely, "That there sound's the laugh of ole' Hoop, visitin' his holler again. Somethings done tickled that funny bone of his."

Today, if you visit Zimmerton and find yourself laughing your head off at something that strikes you as being particularly funny, you just may hear a local citizen whispering to his companion, "Just listen to that, they're hoopin' 'n hollerin', just like ol' Hoop in his holler."

Front Porch Sittin'

Betsy Taylor

Pop (Malcolm Prichard) and Nonna (Eliza Prichard) had worked hard all their lives. Pop apprenticed as a blacksmith at about the time smithing had run its course. He favored training as an auto mechanic, but his father would have none of that. Mr. Prichard insisted that automobiles were certain to be just a flash-in-the-pan, a toy, a fad that would disappear when folks realized they weren't worth the expense and the trouble.

Nonna married Pop when they were eighteen. She set up housekeeping and gave birth to their first son a year and a half later. A confirmed nester, Nonna shone as a homemaker, mother, and wife. Her family was always well-nourished, mostly fed by produce from her garden. A strong believer in balancing meals with fruits, vegetables, and protein, she was a nutritionist before the food pyramid was a glimmer in any scientist's brain.

While she didn't often grant her family's desire for sweets, Nonna became an excellent baker. Most of her treats were sweetened with honey from her own beehives.

Her baked goods soon caught the attention of her neighbors. While Zimmerton had an established bakery in 1910, those bakers fell short when compared to Nonna and the delicacies from her small kitchen.

Naturally Nonna charged for her creations. She undercut the local bakery's prices for her goods by a few cents, a strategy that guaranteed a steady income.

No matter how hard the couple worked each day, they set aside a bit of evening time to visit with each other in their front porch swing. Sometimes they had a minute to themselves, but often a child or two squeezed in between them or balanced on a lap.

You'd think that as motor cars gained popularity leaving horse-drawn vehicles in the dust, a blacksmith's income would dwindle. But in Zimmerton, the demand for repaired metal tools, horseshoes, and gadgets was alive and well. The established notion of replacing a tool if it could be repaired was ridiculed.

Seven years and three more children later the blacksmith shop and its forge closed. Pop, like many young men his age, went off to war.

Zimmerton paid its price for participating in the Great War. The loss of its husbands, sons, and fathers was agonizing. Not one man who returned from the conflict came back unscathed. Bobby Trent came home gasping for breath after breathing mustard gas. He died a few months later. Allen Marshall suffered a head injury that left him prone to tantrums. And Malcolm Prichard returned with only one leg.

Because Nonna grew the food her family ate, they didn't go hungry during the war. None of the kids complained about the scarcity of meat, at least, within hearing distance of their mother. Nonna increased the size of her garden and enlisted the children's help to maintain it. Her chickens provided the family with eggs and, occasionally, stew. She shared with her neighbors and, through the practice of gleaning, kept many of them from starving.

Most of the time, the front porch swing sat empty.

When Pop came home, Nonna added "nurse" to her list of duties. Pop wouldn't reveal the horrors he'd witnessed but, from his nightmare sleep-talk, Nonna absorbed enough to make her shudder.

Bit-by-bit, the couple settled into a new normal. Pop graduated from crutches to a cane when he mastered his artificial leg. He even joked about getting back on his foot instead of back on his feet. The kids laughed and Nonna pretended to. She walked with him on the day he surveyed his shop for the first time.

Her stomach jumped when Pop solemnly looked the place over and said he was finished with smithing. Like a frantic flight of panicked birds, her thoughts collided as they raced around her head. How could they support the children without the shop? What would Pop do with his time? Would he sink into depression like so many of the shell-shocked veterans who were making their way home?

Relief flooded Nonna when Pop continued. "Yep," he said. "This shop will turn into a right nice garage. I'll move the forge to the side." He gestured to an area near the corner. "That'll leave enough room to pull in a car of, say, the size of a Model T."

He stroked Nonna's hand where it rested in the crook of his arm. "That damn war took a lot from me. Only right that I got something back. I learned a lot about repairing cars and trucks. I even worked on a biplane engine. Can you believe that? Don't reckon I'll ever have the chance to do that again."

Pop was wrong about retiring the forge. While he was unable to afford a full set of tools, he was able to craft some that were usable in launching his garage. For fun, he even repaired the porch swing using homemade nails. The economy was recovering, and automobiles were showing up everywhere. Pop kept up with innovations in internal combustion engines and, since Zimmerton was surrounded by farms, he expanded the business to work on farm equipment.

When the two oldest children asked to work in the garage, Pop and Nonna were elated. Pop was a little skeptical when Patricia insisted that the business be named Prichard and Family instead of Prichard and Son. But she had worked alongside her brother during their high school years, and Pop figured she deserved a solid place in the trade she loved.

Pop was wrong about one more thing. In 1929, a fellow knocked on his garage door with a request. He wore a leather helmet with a pair of goggles perched across the top.

"Mr. Prichard," he called out as he scanned the garage. "I've come from the Donnelly farm to ask . . .Oh! There you are."

Pop leaned heavily on his cane as he approached the man who appeared to be a pilot. "Help you, sir?"

"Yes, Mr. Prichard. I believe you can. Mr. Donnelly said you'd be able to fix the engine in my biplane, a WACO. It just up and quit on me. Usually, I can make my own repairs, but . . ." The pilot shook his head as if bewildered.

"Biplane, you say? Well, now I used to be knowledgeable about such things."

The pilot looked hopeful as Pop considered his request.

"Sure would like to take a look under that hood. Maybe I could figure something out." The words were modest, but Pop's eyes sparkled with avarice. The pilot could tell how badly the mechanic wanted to plunge his hands into the plane's engine.

Two hours later when the biplane's engine coughed to life and purred like a well-fed lion, Pop asked, "Where you off to with this old lady?"

"I'm headed west along the National Road. I'll be stopping to sell rides at towns and villages along the way."

"I can't imagine anyone passing up a chance to take a spin," said Pop. "Good luck to you."

"And to you, sir," returned the pilot.

Pop watched his take-off and scanned the sky until the plane was out of sight.

For the next four decades the Prichard children grew, married, and popped out grandchildren turning Malcolm and Eliza into Pop and Nonna. The garage grew into a service station with the children becoming full partners.

In 1962 Malcolm and Eliza had been Pop and Nonna for so long that many of the younger Zimmerton residents believed those to be their given names. The couple were slowing down as their grandchildren took more responsibility for running Pop's Auto Repair. The name of the business had been altered when the first grandchild was born, and business was booming.

Pop was still vigorous having worn out three prosthetic legs. His newest version was of the best quality the VA could provide. The household boasted a TV set and the great grandkids gathered around every Sunday evening at 7:00 pm to watch **Walt Disney's Wonderful World of Color**.

Pop and Nonna kept up with the news, too. They were excited about the prospect of the U.S. launching an astronaut to orbit the Earth.

"Nonna, come quick," called Pop. "That boy from Ohio who's going to space is on TV."

"Oh, the Glenn boy from New Concord." Nonna paused her baking and hurried into the living room as she wiped her hands on a dish towel.

"I understand, Colonel Glenn, that your interest in flight began when you were just a child," said Walter Cronkite.

"Yes, sir," replied Glenn who was 41. "My dad and I were driving along the National Road between Cambridge and New Concord when we passed a WWI biplane in a field. The pilot was charging $5.00 for a ride and Dad asked if I wanted to go up."

"I bet you couldn't wait to take that ride," Cronkite said cheerfully.

"No, sir. That old plane was a WACO. I'm not ashamed to say I scanned her skin for a bullet hole or two. None there."

Cronkite chuckled.

"The rest of the story," continued Glenn, "is that the ride might never have happened if it hadn't been for a fellow in Zimmerton who tinkered with the engine. The pilot told me he was lucky to have broken down at just the right spot."

"That was me!" Pop crowed. "I tinkered. Can you believe it?" Pop was overcome with visions of his place in history.

"Don't get a swelled head, Dear." Nonna squeezed his shoulder.

Pop was still talking excitedly when they bundled up and

adjourned to the front porch swing. As was his habit, he set the swing in motion by pushing with his flesh-and-blood toe. The two held hands while the evening wore on and their voices softened as the conversation gentled.

During their few remaining years Pop and Nonna still worked hard, still helped their grandchildren and great grandchildren, still visited with neighbors who passed by. But they spent more time front porch sittin'.

Years later, a greatgrandchild inherited the house and decided to remodel it. He explained to his mother that he had chosen a more current paint color, planned to change out the dated shutters, and install a trendy metal roof.

Family had been putting it down to wishful thinking and a trick of the breeze when some neighbors reported that, during the evening hours, the swing could be seen to set itself in motion, gliding gently like a pendulum. However, wishful thinking is a powerful emotion.

"You can do what you want now that this is your property," Mom said. "But you'd better, not even for a second, consider touching that front porch swing."

The Farmer Boys
Martha F. Jamail

THE LINDSAY GRAIN and Dairy Farm was located on the outskirts of the town of Zimmerton. There were seven children in the family, all boys, ranging in age from 16 years old to the six-month-old baby.

The older boys were well-trained by their father, Otis, in how to farm the land. Jim, the oldest son, took his job seriously and frequently helped his father work with his younger siblings on their chores.

Otis loved to hunt and often had his loaded 410 shotgun close by on the tractor with him while he was working the field. He was really looking forward to his friends arriving the next day for their big hunting trip. On that day Otis was harvesting his abundant corn crop. The field was so full of corn, Otis had recruited his son, Jim, to help him. They both drove their tractors up and down the loaded fields. It was very cold that day, a good day for harvesting corn since the stalks snap cleanly when they're cold.

After dumping his first load of corn at the mill, Jim returned to the field to get another load when he saw something unusual. His dad's tractor was stopped mid-field, but he didn't see his dad anywhere. He drove his tractor up closer and saw his father slumped over the steering wheel. Jim jumped off his tractor and ran toward his dad, calling out to him. When he got closer, he saw a pool of blood and no response from his father. Jim hurriedly drove his tractor across the fields back to his house to tell his mother the terrible news. They immediately called the emergency squad which arrived very quickly, but sadly had to pronounce his father dead. They determined the tractor had hit a big rut which caused the loaded gun to fall from the seat, and go off, shooting his father in the abdomen.

After the funeral, the family had a meeting and their mother discussed their options. They could sell all their farm equipment and livestock, and move back to town, or stay on the farm and work it as their father had taught them. Jim, being the oldest son, called for a vote which resulted in a unanimous decision to stay on the farm. Their mother, who was a beautician, was relieved to hear that her sons felt dedicated to keeping up the farm their father had enjoyed so much. And Jim, being the oldest, assured his mother that he would work hard with his able brothers to do whatever he could to help them keep their farm.

The high school in Zimmerton was located about ¾ of a mile from their farm, so often, Jim would just drive his tractor to school, and after school, drive the tractor home and right onto the field to work the crops. The teasing he got from fellow students did nothing to deter him.

As time went on, Jim got a job, and the next oldest would help in taking over the responsibilities of the farm. The brothers were able to keep working that way for the next twenty years. Jim stayed on at the farm during that time and acted as a father to his younger siblings.

As they grew, each son graduated and moved into their respective interests. Their mother later moved into the home her father left her. That home was located down the road from the local hospital. The land was expansive, and Jim advised his mother to build a golf course on the property, but his mother and the heirs thought it was too much to take on. They eventually sold the land to a developer who stripped the land of topsoil, and later sold 140 acres of topsoil. The developer also built single-family dwellings and condos. The city of Zimmerton owned the land adjoining them, and they eventually built a golf course.

John, the next oldest son, became a school teacher in Zimmerton, and Harold and Rick went into the pipeline business. Larry got a job with a trucking company, and Denny married into a farming company, and continued the farm. Mike, the youngest, worked as a TV repairman, and later joined Harold and Rick in the pipeline business.

Jim became a service manager in the automotive business. Later he became general manager, then went on to start his own dealership. After 15 years, he closed the business and became successful as a pre-owned car buyer for 20 different dealers.

Jim's mom was very proud of all her sons' successes and assured them their father would have been proud of them too.

Faith and Hope
Claire Cameron

HIRAM WEBSTER HAD BEEN WORKING at the depot since he was 10 years old. After school and during every summer, he was there running errands, delivering packages, giving directions, and making coffee for the station master and Barthalamu LeMasters. Barthalamu's job was to send and receive wires in the telegraph cubicle that adjoined the station master's office. Hiram was close to eighty now, and it was apparent by his faltering eyesight and unsteady gait that this could be his final year doing what he loved most.

Hiram had never married, but lived a quiet life with his sister Irene who was like a mother hen fussing over him as if he were a child. Irene was a retired teacher, widowed at an early age. Although she'd had plenty of opportunities, she had never remarried. Hiram was twenty years old when the previous station master passed away suddenly. Hiram, the most experienced, took the job. Anyone who knew Hiram loved him.

He still wore a boyish grin that made him appear much younger than his 79 years. He'd pass out candy to the children and tease the ladies just to see the color rise in their cheeks.

With every opening and closing, the heavy double doors at the depot protested as they creaked and squeaked. Inside, the many voices of the travelers hummed and buzzed like a nest of busy bees. Some waited for the train to take them to their destinations. Then there were those who stepped off the train asking for directions to the hotel or where they could get a good meal. For others who waited for a relative or friend to pick them up, men and boys carried crates of goods and hurriedly unloaded their heavy burdens on the dock as they mopped the sweat running into their eyes.

It was due to all the hustle and bustle that the station master failed to notice the frail old lady slip out the door and back onto the train leaving behind some precious cargo.

At 7pm sharp the last train of the day left the depot chugging and chortling leaving puffs of black smoke behind. Those passengers departing on the evening train could be seen brushing dust from their dresses and hats with bellies growling long overdue for a hot meal and comfortable bed. They could be heard greeting friends and family ready for a short car ride to the nearest hotel.

Ten minutes or so after the last of the travelers departed, Hiram finished up his work tallying ticket sales and counting the cash in the drawer. Carefully placing the cash in the safe, he turned the lock on the door. His eyes, tired from the long day, he switched off the office lamp and breathed a weary sigh. As he closed and locked his office door behind him, the old lights in the waiting area cast eerie shadows over the well-worn benches. Hiram had to look twice to be sure his eyes weren't playing tricks on him.

There lying asleep on the bench on his left were two little girls with blonde curls.

He approached them quietly so as not to frighten them. His thoughts were racing. How did they get here? And with whom? Where did they come from? What am I to do? Hiram was afraid to wake them.

Irene, he thought. Call Irene. She'll know what to do.

Reaching into his pocket, he pulled out his keys. They jingle-jangled as he fumbled around to find the key to the office. Once he reached his phone, it only took only two minutes to get his sister on the phone. Beads of perspiration sprang up on his forehead. Absent-mindedly he wiped it with his clean white handkerchief. His voice was shaking as he explained his dilemma to Irene. She relieved his mind by telling him she'd be right there after she fetched the doc. Hiram didn't understand how the doc could help, but he was all for any help he could get.

Doc and Irene arrived, and the three of them came up with a plan to care for the girls until their family could be located. Irene gently woke the girls whispering encouraging words to them. "Hi, girls, I'm Irene. This is Doc. We came to meet you. Can you tell us your names?"

Both girls spoke at once. "Fahothp," was the garbled reply.

Irene smiled and softly tapped one child on her shoulder. "Let's start with you. What is your name?"

"Faith," the girl wearing a head of curls replied.

"And your name, dear?" Irene asked as she smiled at the girl's twin. "Hope," was the other child's reply.

"You did very well, young ladies. Now we're going to do our best to find your family. But first, Dr. Rob wants to be sure you're not ill, so he's going to look at your eyes and throats. He's very gentle and will have a treat for you when he's finished. Okay?"

Both girls nodded and sat very still while Doc looked them over for any sign of illness or abuse and gave them a clean bill of health. When they were finished, he pulled two suckers from his pocket and handed one to each. The girls eagerly accepted the treat and thanked Doc properly. Although both girls had red eyes from crying and, apparently, long hours of travel, they appeared to have been well-cared-for. Irene and Hiram were going to take them home and give them supper and a comfortable bed for the night.

Tomorrow, word would be sent around town to seek help in identifying the little ones. Mr. LeMasters would send telegrams to surrounding towns hoping to get information about who the girls belonged to. The train conductors on yesterday's trains would be questioned for information about anyone traveling with the curly-haired children. Doc drove Irene, Hiram, and the girls home with the promise of checking in with them tomorrow.

Once home, Irene heated up a dinner of fried chicken, potato salad, and baked beans. The girls ate well, mouths full of warm cocoa with fresh whipped cream. Hiram, his belly full and worn out from the long day and harrowing evening was shooed off to bed.

After washing hands and faces, Irene gently changed the girls from dresses to nightgowns. Although Irene was a little lady, she was certain the twins would swim in her camisoles. But, to her surprise, when she removed their dresses, both girls had notes pinned to their little white slips. A tear slid down her cheek when she read the first one.

My name is Faith it read. I will be five years old in July. I was born July 4, 1975. My Mama is on her way to heaven. Before she left, she kissed me good-bye and asked Miss Anna to bring me and Sissy to Zimmerton. She said she knew someone here would give us a good home because Zimmerton is full of good people. Miss Anna couldn't keep us because she is too old. She said God will bless whoever gives us a good home.

The other note read the same except to say that this child's name is Hope and that Hope is 7 minutes older than Faith. The note further implored the finder to keep the children together.

Each girl carried a small drawstring bag. One was ruby red and the other was sapphire blue. Each contained an initialed handkerchief embroidered with a tiny rose. Faith's bag held a little cross studded with ruby rhinestones. Hope's bag held the same kind of cross studded with sapphire rhinestones. In each bag Irene found a photo of the two of them. In the picture they were about three years old posed with a blond-haired woman with a beautiful smile. The resemblance was unmistakable. The woman had to have been their mother. The names Mercy, Faith, and Hope were written on the photo's back.

Irene shook her head, wiped her cheek, and put each note into her dress pocket. Tucking both girls into bed with homemade

Faith and Hope

dolls they'd carried, she softly kissed each forehead. "Angel kisses from your Mama," she told them. "I'll be right across the hall."

Leaving a night light on, Irene tip-toed out the door. In her room, she knelt beside the bed and folded her hands in prayer. She asked the Lord to give her the strength and guidance she'd need to carry out the wishes of their mother and find the children good parents. With a word of thanks, she climbed into bed. Weariness overtook her, but she rested peacefully believing her prayers would be answered.

Two months had passed since the night Irene had taken in the curly-topped twins. Surrounding towns had been contacted and pictures of the girls and their mama had been sent. Pleas for information about the family had been sought. Newspapers within a hundred-mile radius carried their story in hopes that someone would come forward. Conductors and railway workers were questioned. It was as if the girls had appeared out of nowhere and no one knew a thing about them.

Days turned into months with no leads about relatives or even acquaintances of the adorable little girls. Hiram doted on them, playing hide-and-seek, treating them to ice cream, and spoiling them every chance he got. Irene made name tags for them so that they'd be able to tell them apart. The whole town had taken the children under their wing, but the young pastor of the First Baptist Church and his wife had grown especially fond of them. The couple was unable to have children of their own. The members of their congregation suspected that they would soon be celebrating an adoption.

On Sunday July 1, the announcement of a birthday celebration to be held on July 4 was announced. Pastor Fitzgerald and his wife, Caroline, would host it in the churchyard. On the morning of July 3, Irene packed the girls' belongings and waited for the pastor in the parlor.

When she heard the car pull up, Irene took the girls by the

hand and walked them onto the porch. The girls ran to greet the arrivals. Reverend Fitz asked them if they would like to live with him and Caroline forever. They would be the girls' mama and papa.

Both girls jumped up and down shouting questions. "Forever?" "Really?" "Our own mama and papa forever?"

Hope hugged Caroline and Faith and put her arms around Reverend Fitz. "Yes, yes, yes!" they crowed in unison.

"Miss Irene, I love you," Hope said as she ran into Irene's arms.

"I will miss you," Faith said, "but we have to go now. You are very nice and have been so good to us. But I think you may be too old to keep up with us."

Irene laughed as she gave each one an understanding hug and kiss.

"I'll just get their bags and give you a break. For the life of me, I can't understand how you managed to keep up with these two," Reverend Fitz commented casting a sympathetic look at Irene.

"With the help of the Lord and my brother, we did fairly well, don't you think?"

They all chuckled as the reverend loaded the bags, and Caroline tucked the girls into the back seat. "And we're off," shouted Caroline. "See you at the party, Irene. Don't forget Hiram."

Irene waved until they were out of sight. She made her way back to the house giving thanks that her prayers had been answered.

The 4th of July was hot, but a steady breeze made the day more comfortable. Faith and Hope were the center of attention in their new dresses and party hats. They played tag and jumped rope with the other children.

Around one o'clock, the reverend called for quiet and blessed the food. "Before we eat, Caroline and I would like you all to know how thankful we are for each and every one of you. Since

Faith and Hope

we came to Zimmerton you have all been kind and gracious to us, treating us like family. Thank you so much for supporting us and embracing and building up our church."

"Now, it's our pleasure to introduce the newest members of our family, our officially adopted daughters, Faith and Hope."

"We had so much hope and abundant faith. We asked, and they were given to us to love as our own forever. Thank you all for loving them, too."

"Now, let's chow down. But save room for cake and ice cream."

Everyone clapped and congratulated Reverend Fitz and Caroline before lining up at the buffet. Soon the meal was over, and the congregation was served cake and ice cream. After dessert, the girls were ushered to the gift able. "Okay, girls, take turns opening your gifts and, don't forget to thank the givers as you open each one," Caroline said. "Hope, you're the oldest, so please let your younger sister go first."

Hope frowned but decided it would be the kind thing to do. Faith opened her first gift, a necklace with a heart on it. When she tried to put it on, she discovered that she needed the help of her new mama. "Thank you, Miss Irene and Hiram," she said warmly.

Hope accepted her package and found that it contained a similar gift. She also went to Caroline for help. The gifts were opened one at a time and thanks were given as each was unwrapped until the last two packages lay on the table. The package with Faith's name contained a dark blue dress with velvet ribbon around the collar. The other package that bore Hope's name contained a red dress with red velvet lacing.

"I think that blue dress is mine, Faith," said Hope.

"No, it's mine," Faith replied.

The argument continued until Reverend Fitz intervened. "Whoa, girls. It's getting late. Thank everyone for the lovely gifts. We'll sort this out after our guests depart."

With pouting lips, the girls mumbled their thanks. Embarrassed, Caroline apologetically added her thanks to their friends for making the day special. Taking their hands, she ushered the girls into their new home leaving her husband to say the good-byes.

Their father walked in as they sat on the sofa dark circles shadowing their eyes. Caroline had finished cleaning and joined them.

"Ladies, I'm very disappointed today by the way you acted in front of your guests. Would you mind telling your mother what caused your bickering?"

"I always get the blue stuff," Hope answered. "And Faith always gets the red."

"That's not true," piped up Faith.

"Yes, it is," shouted Hope.

"Okay, girls. Calm down," said Caroline.

But the argument continued until neither Reverend Fitz nor Caroline could remember who got which color. Neither could they be certain who told the truth. The couple stared at each other. "What do we do now?" they said simultaneously. The couple decided to sleep and pray on the matter. By that time the girls were so tired they had stopped fussing at each other.

When faces and hands had been washed, teeth brushed, nighties put on, prayers said, and good-night kisses given, Caroline and William left the room. Once the parents left, the girls turned to each other.

Hope smiled and whispered, "We sure tricked them, didn't we?"

"We sure did," Faith answered. "Just like we did back home."

Caroline gave a sigh of relief as she turned off her bedside lamp and laid her head on her pillow. Turning to her husband she asked softly, "Do you think it will get any easier?"

"Do you mean, telling them apart? I can't see that it makes much difference."

"No, learning who's telling the truth."

"That's a much more important matter. They're only five. We have time to work on it."

Caroline closed her eyes to pray for wisdom and strength. Little did she realize how much of both she would need.

Bossy and Her Hill

Mark Cooper

NINE-YEAR-OLD MOLLY JOHNSON SHIVERED in the back seat of her mom's new Tesla as Sally flipped on the turn signal and made a right onto the twisting road leading down the steep hill. "Mom, why do we always take this road? I don't like it!"

"Yes dear, but it's the quickest way into Zimmerton. Besides, coasting down the hill saves the battery."

"But why does it have to be so steep and twisty? It's scary!"

Her mom smiled. "You see the name on the road sign? 'Bossy's Hill'?" Well, close your eyes and let me tell you about your great-great-great grandfather Chester's cow, Bossy...."

* * *

NO QUESTION ABOUT IT, 'Ol Bossy was in charge. Whatever part of the pasture she chose to graze in, the rest of the herd would quickly follow. Bossy was the first to find a weakness in the fence and push through so the herd could enjoy the greener grass on the other side. If a coyote, dog, or even a groundhog, made itself visible, Bossy would shake her head, snort, stomp her hooves, and lead the charge of bovines to chase away the intruder.

Bossy also thought she ruled over people. If anyone other than old farmer Chester came into the pasture, she was liable to stomp her hooves and start moving in their direction menacingly. But she seemed to like old Chester. With a lifetime of farming experience under his belt, he understood and respected animals. The years had taken a toll on his knees and hips, he had to use a walking stick for stability as he trekked over the rough pasture. Bossy knew he'd never consider using the stick to strike his cattle.

When Chester put out hay and grain for the livestock, he'd talk to them, cracking corny jokes that he made up on the spur of the moment. "Why'd the cow crawl under the moon? Because she couldn't jump over it!!!"

Then he'd look at Bossy and wink. "That was a pretty bad one wasn't it, girl?" She'd give him an arrogant look and flick her tail. Chester would grin, "Girl, you're the dang stubbornest old cow. But you make gittin' out here every day worthwhile for me." Then he'd dig in his pocket and pull out a special treat he'd made from grain and molasses. "Now, don't you tell the others you're gittin' this, because this is just for you!" He'd give her an affectionate grin, and, once in a while, he could have sworn she grinned back.

Each time Chester needed to move the cattle from the valley pasture up to the hilltop or into the barn lot, he'd call out, "OK Bossy, where are ya? Let's go girl!" With a toss of her head and that flick of her tail just to show him she couldn't be forced, Bossy trotted his direction, the rest of the herd following close behind.

Using his stick for support, Chester always led the cattle across the long valley to the shallow upper end. This path was reasonably easy for the old farmer to navigate. Although Bossy knew she could save time by going up the steep side of the hill, she never contested Chester's lead. She figured he'd earned the right to take whatever path he wanted.

The day came when Chester didn't show up to the field. Instead, that young whippersnapper Chet the Third came out to call for the cattle and move them to the upper pasture. He believed animals needed to know who was boss. So, he threw his arms around in the air and yelled obscenities at the cows to get them moving. Slowly, reluctantly, the herd began to respond. All but

Bossy, she hung back and eyed the cows taking their usual path, traipsing across the valley and up the shallow side of the hill. Then she turned her head and looked at the steepest part of the hill that they had been grazing right next to. She had been yearning to take this part of the hill for years. Now that old Chester wasn't here, she'd do it! With her infamous tail flick, she took off. Her hooves stirred up puffs of dust as she made her way up the hill, putting more and more distance between herself and Chet, who was now turning the air blue swearing at her. When he and the rest of the herd finally arrived at the upper pasture gate, Bossy was already there, waiting with a smirk on her face. From that day forward, Bossy ignored Chet's directions and continued making her own way up the hill, even though none of the other cattle followed her lead.

The weather turned cold. On a particularly miserable day Chet needed to move the cattle up the hill to the barn lot. A winter storm was brewing, and it would be far safer to feed and shelter them there. Intent on getting the job done quickly so he could get back into his warm farmhouse, he flapped his arms and yelled louder than ever, "Come on you stupid cows! Get moving if you know what's good for ya!"

That was it! Bossy wasn't going to let anyone call her and her fellow bovines stupid cows. She let out a such a bellow that the rest of the herd knew they'd better pay attention to her. She ran towards the path that she'd been forming up the steep hillside. The other cattle quickly followed, surrendering once again to Bossy's leadership.

"NO! NO! NO!" Chet screamed. He lost his breath trying to keep up. But what was worse, as he scrambled up the steep hill behind the herd, he stepped in a fresh cow patty that Bossy had thoughtfully placed. He slid, went down hard, and tumbled over and over before finally being stopped by a thorn bush.

When he finally arrived at the barn lot gate, filthy, stinky, and panting, the cattle were already there. They looked at him as if to say, "Where have you been slow poke?" Bossy had a contented look on her face, and a gleam in her eye. Chet knew he was defeated.

From that day on, the cattle followed Bossy rather than him. She always led her herd up the path that she'd made, a path that wound up and down, threading around big rocks, circumventing low-hanging tree branches, and avoiding prickly brush. And poor Chet kept doing his best to keep up. This was no path made for humans, but just right for sure-footed cattle.

Eventually Chet, now older and wiser, began using that path when he would ride his horse from the farm into the small village of Zimmerton. After all, the cow path was a short cut, and no challenge for his sure-footed steed. He also gave some neighbors permission to ride their horses along the same path when they went into town. The more it was used, the wider the path grew until Chet decided he could probably drive his cart on it. That saved a lot of time when he needed to go for supplies at the village's general store. And again, he let his neighbors do the same. "It's not very wide and its awfully steep," Chet cautioned them, "But if'n you're wantin' to go to town the shortest way, Bossy's path is quicker than the other way around the hill!"

Model Ts began showing up in Zimmerton and the surrounding countryside. Chet just shook his head the day his son bought his own Model T truck home to the farm. One day the young man looked over Bossy's path, "Hmm... this is awfully rough. But it'd shave off a lot of time if I could take my truck on it when I go into town. I'm gonna give it a try!" He tried, and he made it.

Chet, now a county commissioner, persuaded his fellow commissioners to pay to have Bossy's path improved. They hired a bunch of young, strong country boys to bring their picks and shovels and widen the path. Next, wagon loads of crushed stone from the quarry were brought in to form a roadbed. Chet's young grandson, having heard the story of Bossy all his life, even painted a sign on an old board, "Bossy's Hill." Bossy's path was now an official shortcut to Zimmerton, a steep, twisting shortcut that anyone could use, if they dared.

* * *

"Wow Mom! Did great-great-great grandpa's cow really make this road?" Mollie gasped as her mom finished the tale.

"Well, that's what people claim, dear. Now, open your eyes and look where we are. We've made it to the bottom of Bossy's Hill!"

Gypsy Wagon Comes to Town
Beverly Wencek Kerr

SPRING HAD ARRIVED IN THE SMALL TOWN of Zimmerton in 1930. That meant that adults were out plowing their gardens and children were enjoying the freedom of being outside. Imagine their surprise when they heard the tinkling of bells and a colorful wagon pulled into town drawn by two beautiful horses.

Everyone stopped what they were doing as the wagon moved to the gazebo in the middle of town. Most had never seen a wagon so beautifully decorated and were curious as to who these people were.

But Mayor Lucious McCallister knew. As soon as he heard the bells, he recalled seeing a similar wagon when he was a child. The gypsy's wagon was their most prized possession as these wanderers needed a home they could take with them wherever they went. The outside was decorated with paintings of things they enjoyed, such as horses, dogs, birds, flowers, and elaborate scrollwork.

Lucious remembered his parents telling him, "Stay away from that Gypsy Wagon! They will try to steal things and sometimes even children." So, he quickly moved to the gazebo and told the wanderers they were not welcome in town.

The gypsies were used to this kind of treatment and graciously moved to the outskirts of town where they found a friendly family, George and Mary Byers, who would permit them to camp on their farm. Many thought Mary Byers was a psychic so perhaps she would enjoy associating with the fortune teller that would most likely be part of the Gypsy Wagon.

Wherever Gypsy Wagons are found, there was usually a

woman who told fortunes and provided the main source of income for their family. Her husband sold or traded horses or jewelry. Their daughters were trained at an early age to become either fortune tellers or beggars while sons received training to help their fathers sell and trade. Since many believed the gypsies were swindlers, it became common that to say that to cheat someone was to "gyp" them.

This family consisted of the husband Ladin (short for Alladin because he was considered magical), Naomi, his wife, and their two brightly dressed children – a boy and a girl named Kaven and Miri. Ladin was a man of large stature. Heavy weight showed wealth, power, and strength in the gypsy world.

It wasn't unusual for these wagons to frequent the backroads of the countryside, so Zimmerton seemed a perfect place to set up camp for a few days. That first evening at the Byers farm, Ladin got out his violin and played some lively music around the campfire. Kaven and Miri produced a hypnotic accompanying beat using brass vases, spoons, and castanets while Naomi danced around the campfire.

Bonnie, Virginia, and Frank, the Byers children, sat on their porch and listened to the music for a while but eventually crept a little closer. They enjoyed the added excitement in their small town. Bonnie and Virginia enjoyed the bright colors that the gypsies wore as well as all their pretty jewelry. They watched and listened until their mother called them home for bedtime.

The next morning, they were up bright and early to visit the gypsy camp. This time Mary went with them as she had a desire to have her fortune told. The cost at that time was a quarter so she felt they could spare that much.

As she approached the camp, the fortune teller said, "You have beautiful children. I wish they were mine." Frank and Virginia hid behind their mother's skirt, but Bonnie wasn't the least bit afraid.

When Mary gave the quarter to Gypsy Naomi, she was invited inside the wagon, the door was closed, and the children had to wait outside.

When Mary came back outside, she had a smile on her face but wouldn't tell anyone what Naomi had said. "Come on, children, let's go back to the house and we can come back this evening when they have the campfire going."

Naomi took her children by the hand and decided to walk with her husband to the Mercantile in Zimmerton to buy a few things they needed. She also hoped to encourage people to visit her family as they depended on non-gypsies as their customers. Whenever she found someone who had any interest, she had some hand-made cards that she gave them to welcome them to their campsite.

Laden had heard that Zimmerton Tire & Magnets had copper bracelets for sale. Those bracelets could cure many things, especially arthritis, and would be profitable on future gypsy road trips. Perhaps they would trade him some bracelets for painting their garage where the paint was faded and peeling.

"Hello, Ned, could I see the copper bracelets you have for sale? We like to use them and have many friends who use them too." Laden began the conversation.

"Well, I suppose it wouldn't do any harm to let you look, but I'll be keeping an eye on you," the shopkeeper told him. He knew gypsies were not to be trusted.

"Thanks," Laden said with a smile, "I promise I won't take anything."

Ned showed Laden the bracelets and told him they were 25 cents each. Hmm! Laden thought, That's just the price of Naomi telling a fortune.

"Could we make a trade?" asked Laden. "Your building looks like it could use a coat of paint. How many bracelets could you give me if I painted your shop?"

"Let me see." Ned was thinking, "I'll give you ten for sure and maybe more if you do a good job. I have the paint inside but never found anyone to paint the building for me."

While Laden was making that deal, Naomi was busy talking to the ladies in town at Martha's Place and The Corner Store. She even talked to Rachel, the mayor's wife, and invited her to their campground. Of course, when Rachel went home, she told her husband, "The Gypsy Lady was in town today passing out information about things they had for sale or trade."

"Don't you go near them. Do you hear me? They are nothing but trouble," was the mayor's response.

That evening the Byers family gathered at the Gypsy Camp around the campfire to listen to the music and their exciting tales of life on the road. It was no surprise that a few of the townsfolk quietly stood on the outskirts of the camp to listen and observe. No one saw anything that appeared to be a problem and they did enjoy the music.

The following morning Bonnie headed over to the camp to talk to Miri. Bonnie led her along a dirt road known to locals as Bossy's Hill hoping Miri would tell her more about the gypsy life.

Bonnie began questioning, "What do you like to eat when you are traveling?"

"We usually eat two meals a day – one in the morning and the other late afternoon. Mom makes a delicious stew in a pot over the campfire. Sometimes she fixes cabbage rolls as a treat and bakes them in the campfire coals."

"How long will you stay here?" Bonnie wanted to know.

Miri wasn't certain but told her, "Usually we stay in one place for about a week, or less if people are unfriendly and ask us to leave."

"Can you tell fortunes like your mom?"

"Mom is teaching me how to tell fortunes by connecting with the people. After a while, you get to know a lot about a person just by watching them and listening."

"Oh, Miri, do you think you could tell my fortune?"

"Bonnie, I could try but Mom would do it better." Miri began by closing her eyes and thinking about Bonnie. "I feel like you are looking for excitement in life and may find it soon."

"You are certainly right about my liking excitement." Bonnie smiled as they continued walking back to the gypsies' campsite.

The days went by with many ladies coming to get their fortunes told by Naomi. One day there was a surprise visitor, Rachel, the mayor's wife. She asked Naomi to tell her what was in her future.

Naomi was pleased and surprised by the visit but tried to treat her as she would any other customer. So, she took her inside the wagon for a reading. "Would you mind letting me hold your necklace so I can get a better connection with you?"

Rachel was a little afraid to let the gypsy hold her necklace, but she finally handed it over.

Naomi closed her eyes as she felt the necklace, then told her, "You have had a difficult life always trying to please someone else. It is time that you do the things you enjoy in life. Don't let yourself be controlled by others. Remember your husband is not always right. I see much happiness in your future if you follow your heart."

Tears formed in Rachel's eyes. She knew exactly what Naomi was talking about. The mayor always tried to control her. Was she strong enough to withstand his control? Maybe it was possible.

"Thanks, Naomi. I appreciate your telling me that. I hope you have a safe journey wherever you are headed." At that, Rachel left the Gypsy Wagon and headed back home.

Bonnie and Miri continued their daily walks. Each time Bonnie learned a little more about the excitement of the gypsy life.

"How do gypsies cure a headache? My mom gets them all the time, and nothing seems to help."

Bonnie told her, "When my mom has a headache, she wraps up slices of potato with a scarf and places them on her forehead.

If we don't have any potatoes, she uses tea leaves in the same way. We always have tea leaves!"

"Wow! I'll have to tell Mom about those methods. Thanks. What does she give you for a cold?"

"Sometimes, Mom boils brown sugar and gives me a spoonful, or if the cold is really bad, she dices up an onion and squeezes the juice out of the pieces then adds a little sugar. It really helps."

These remedies were very interesting to Bonnie. She could hardly wait to tell her mom what she had found out.

The week went by quickly, too quickly for Bonnie. Miri told her they would be leaving the next day early in the morning since her dad had finished painting the garage at Zimmerton Tire and received the copper bracelets. That evening they sat around the campfire, sang songs, and said their goodbyes.

Early the next morning, Mary fixed a breakfast of pancakes, a favorite of Bonnie's, because she knew how much Bonnie would be missing her new friend, Miri. "Children, it's breakfast time," she called up the stairway. Down ran Frank and Virginia, but no Bonnie. "Where's Bonnie?" said a puzzled mom.

"She's not in her room," answered Virginia, "so she must be outside already."

Mom called out the door, "Bonnie, I've got pancakes for you." Still no answer. "Where could that girl be?"

Frank smirked, "Maybe the gypsies stole her!"

That didn't make Mary smile. "Oh, my! Could it be? I remember the fortune teller told me that she wished my beautiful children were hers. I'll have to go to town and see if anyone saw them leave." First, they checked carefully around their farm to make sure Bonnie wasn't somewhere crying over her friend's departure.

Well, the town was in an uproar. The mayor said, "I told you those gypsies were up to no good. Why won't you listen to me? Now we have lost a child." Everyone came to comfort the Byers family, but they could not be comforted. Finally, they decided to go home and search again outside to see if they could find Bonnie.

All of a sudden, George heard the sound of bells. It sounded like the Gypsy Wagon. Sure enough, there it came down the road to their house. Naomi hopped out of the wagon and told them, "I'm bringing your daughter back home. She hid away in our wagon. She said she wanted to be a gypsy, too. When we found her, I told her she had to return home for now. Perhaps someday she could be a gypsy but not now."

The Byers family was so happy to have Bonnie back that they didn't even scold her. George went to town and told everyone how Bonnie had returned. He pointed out to the mayor, "See, gypsies aren't bad. They brought Bonnie back to us." Mayor McCallister grumbled but his wife had to smile. Sometimes her husband was wrong just like Naomi had said.

Over supper that evening, Bonnie told the family, "I'm sorry I worried you. Someday I am going to be a gypsy. You wait and see." Maybe her wish will come true.

Miracle on Goodyear Road
Samuel D. Besket

THE FROZEN SNOW CRUNCHED like broken glass under Jason's boots as he trudged half-awake toward his truck. Pulling himself into the cab, he started the engine and briefly rested his head on the steering wheel. Just a few minutes ago he'd had a cup of hot chocolate in his hand as he waited for Monday Night Football to come on, when the phone rang.

"Don't answer it," he'd shouted to his wife. "Sue, I'm done for the day." He heard her talking in the next room and knew his day wasn't over. A few minutes later she walked into the room. Standing in the doorway arch, she paused.

"It's Aunt Liz... her furnace won't come on."

Jason Schmidt and his wife Sue owned Zimmerton Heating and Cooling. The last month had been brutal with service calls.

The eastern half of the United States was gripped in the coldest winter in decades. The jet stream had suddenly dipped south clearing a path for a polar vortex to dump sub-zero temperatures and snow, paralyzing the eastern half of the country. Later, it would be called "The Blizzard of 78."

Aunt Liz, a spry ninety-three-year-old spinster, lived on her grandfather's farm about two miles from town. She was the last survivor among her eleven siblings. For years Jason had tried to get her to sell the farm and move to town. The answer was always the same, "Maybe next year. Grandfather was one of the Zimmerton founding fathers. I just can't leave."

Jason stomped snow off his boots as he walked up the front steps. Aunt Liz held the door open and ushered him in.

"Who shoveled your walk?" he asked.

"A nice young man from the township", she said. "They were checking on senior citizens. He even fixed my furnace. It was only the breaker."

With a stunned look, Jason asked. "Why didn't you call me?"

"I tried, but your wife answered. You left your phone beside your chair."

Jason felt his pocket and, sure enough, it was empty.

"Well, sit for a spell. I have some hot tea on the stove, Give me your coat."

Later, as he was leaving, he noticed that his was only one set of tire tracks coming up the drive. How could that be? he thought. Maybe Aunt Liz was confused. But who shoveled her walk?

Finally, when Jason was back home watching Monday Night Football, Sue handed him a fresh cup of hot chocolate.

"Sue, can you come in here?"

"Just a minute, I still have a few dishes to wash."

Jason couldn't wait. He followed her to the kitchen. "I think Aunt Liz is losing it," he said. "Her furnace was working fine. She said a young man from the township fixed it for her. But there weren't any tracks in her driveway."

"Well, she is ninety-three. It may be just a case of cabin fever. She sounded fine on the phone."

The temperatures warmed during the following week and Jason's workload eased. But, he was stymied by the incident at Aunt Liz's house.

"You're home early," Sue said as she greeted him at the door.

"This issue with Aunt Liz is bugging me. According to the gas company, the gas line running along Goodyear Road did freeze up last Monday. Something about a filter at the compressor station. But who is this mystery man?"

"You need to read the headline in today's newspaper," she said.

Mystery Man Checks on Residents Along Goodyear Road

During Recent Blizzard. Local Officials Are Unable to Identify the Man or Where he Came From.

When questioned by officials, one elderly lady said he was an angel, and another gentleman thought he was from outer space.

"Now I'm more confused," Jason said. "One lady thinks we have angels walking around in blizzards and another fellow thinks he was an alien."

The weather continued to warm, and by the middle of February, all traces of the blizzard were gone. But the bizarre incident with Aunt Liz lingered in his mind. Finally, he went to the police station and talked to the dispatcher.

"The mayor had us go door to door trying to figure out who this mystery man is. We visited over thirty homes. Everyone gave the same answer. He was a nice young man from the township. Here is another puzzling statement. They all said he was there at the same time, 9:45 pm."

Now, more befuddled than ever, Jason decided to call it a day and go home.

"You're home early," Sue said. "I'll fix your supper, then I'm going to Bible study. The paper is on your stand, and I got you some chips."

"Well, if you don't mind, I would like to go with you."

Sue took off her apron and gave him a big hug. "Looks like this really is the season for miracles."

Zimmerton Mercantile
Claire Cameron

IT WAS 1930 AND HARD TIMES were just beginning. Although the Carlisles were very careful with their spending, during the depression people were finding it difficult to make a living and survive. It wasn't easy keeping the Mercantile stocked since not only was money scarce, but so were products. Many of the good people of Zimmerton were barely holding on, unable to purchase necessities and often times the proprietor of the Mercantile was asked to barter or take an IOU rather than be paid in cash for his goods. But life went on and so did the daily routine.

The big glass windows advertised a sale on fresh fruit. Bushel baskets of peaches, pears, apples, along with pints of mouth-watering strawberries and black and red raspberries, made for a colorful summer display. In the other window, Granny Matilda Carlisle proudly displayed her handmade quilts. Nine-patch, wedding ring, log cabin to name just a few. And scattered here and there in the window were sewing notions, plain and printed fabric and brightly colored ribbon.

It was hotter than normal for this time of year. Most all of Zimmerton relied on the electricity to hold out while their old fans whirred with blades spinning like windmills on a windy day.

Rocking back and forth, the ancient black metal fan in the Mercantile began walking across the old wooden floor like it had legs of its own. Just about a foot away was Gracie Mae the Carlisle's granddaughter. She was a wispy little girl with long auburn braids. Muttering to herself she grabbed the handle of the metal creature and moved it back to where it had begun its walk.

Determined for it not to happen again she laid two bricks that were used for door stops in front of the metal cradle attached to the fan. "There, take that you devil!" she exclaimed. It was blistering hot, she thought as she wiped her forehead with the handkerchief that she drew from her pocket. As if to taunt her, the fan began to squeal like a pig caught in a briar patch.

She gave the "thing" her best scowl and stuck her tongue out at it. "I don't have time for you, you freak! I hate you and if you die on me now I will cut your cord and dig you a deep grave!"

Trying to ignore the squealing and rattling, Gracie went back to taking the jars off and wiping down the shelves in Granddad's store.

Gracie would be twelve in November. Her grandparents took her in after her daddy died and her mama went to the hospital for the mentally ill. Although young, she took on the duties she was given seriously and loved helping out in the Mercantile. Her mind was always busy. A pretty and obedient child, she had a curiosity about everything you could think of. Unfortunately, her desire for adventure could bring her trouble on occasion. Gracie was forever asking Granddaddy Adam, better known as Ad, questions. His knowledge made him her hero. Not only did he spoil her, but she knew whatever she had questions about he'd have a good answer.

Ad Carlisle made his way down the three steps into the store, his cane going thump, thump, thump. He'd nearly lost his leg in an accident due to his fondness for moonshine, but the near loss, along with his wife's threats of divorce, ended his drinking days. "Why is it so dog-gone hot out here, Gracie? And what is that squealing?" Granddaddy asked, frowning.

With an annoyed look on her face, Gracie answered, "Maybe because that fan turned into the ole devil spitting out sparks and walking on its own! Then the blades will quit for a while then they start up again."

"If that's so then, better shut it down and fetch the tinker to take a look at it," Granddaddy said while shaking his head.

Thinking this would be a nice time to break away from chores for a bit, Gracie unplugged the fan, took off her apron, hung it on the wooden coat rack and ran off. The old screen door slammed shut as she went.

Granddaddy was just beginning to wonder what was taking Gracie so long when it was only a half mile to the Tinker's when she came sailing through the door with a handful of wildflowers and a dozen fresh eggs. "Now I see what took you so long, girlie. You've been out pickin' flowers again, haven't ya?"

"They're for Granny, Granddaddy. You know what kind of flower this is?" Before he could answer, Gracie went on. "And this one, and this one? And how's come roses are the only ones with thorns?"

Granddaddy smiled and said, "Gracie Mae if you give me a chance, I will answer you! The yellow flowers are buttercups, the blue ones are bluebell's, the yellow ones with the black middle are Black-eyed Susans. The roses have thorns to keep animals from eating them. They're the only flower that smells so sweet that they think they are the only ones that need those spikey thorns."

"Oh, that's good to know," said Gracie grinning from cheek to cheek. "I gotta go give these eggs to Granny."

"Well, you do that, sunshine, then back here to finish the shelves."

"Yes, I will, Granddaddy and Tinker's busy, but he said he'll be here right after dinner."

Granddaddy nodded and turned back to his newspaper shaking his head. That girl sure is full of questions, he thought.

Granny turned away from the heat of the stove as Gracie came skipping through the kitchen doorway.

"Granny, Tinker's wife sent you these eggs. She'd like to trade them for some of your sassafras tea and some honey if you can spare it," she said.

Granny smiled thinking of her friend Sadie, Tinker's wife.

"How's she look, Gracie?" Granny knew Sadie wasn't well. Just last week, she'd passed out while hanging out her laundry. It was a blessing Tinker found her when he did as he'd just returned from fixing the pie cooler at Martha's Place. Though she wasn't hurt in the fall, Doc had taken her blood to be tested.

"Mrs. Tinker looked white and had dark circles under her eyes, Granny, but she smiled her pretty smile and gave me a slice of her homemade bread with strawberry jam. Mmm, was it good!" Granny gave Gracie a worried look. "Well, I guess I'll be going over after supper to see if I can help her with anything," Granny said.

"Close your eyes, please Granny, I got you something."

When Granny opened her eyes, they sparkled with delight. "Wildflowers for me? Well, you are the kindest girl I know, Gracie Mae." Granny spoke softly and planted a kiss on Gracie's forehead.

"Granny, how many eggs can a chicken lay in one day? And how can a baby chick be in an egg? And Granny, how can you tell if the baby chick is a boy or girl? How do you know what egg you can eat and which one has a chick in it?"

Gracie was close to popping another question when Granny said, "Grace, those are best answered by Grandad. Now please go and ask him while I finish up supper."

"Yes, ma'am," was Gracie's reply as she skipped out the door, down the steps and back into the store where she stood facing her Grandaddy.

Feeling her presence, he smiled. "What is it, Gracie?"

"Well, Grandad, I have a question."

"Just one question, is it?"

"Well, I guess there's more, Gracie replied. What I need to know is—."

Grandad chuckled as Gracie sputtered out the same questions she'd asked her Granny. Before he replied a thought crossed his mind. "Did your Granny send you to me for your answers, Gracie?"

"That she did, and it's 'cause she thinks you're smarter than she is."

"Is that a fact?"

"That it is, Grandaddy."

"Well, put that apron of yours on and finish the shelves while I try to answer them for you."

It was going on 7:00 pm when Tinker came through the door whistling a tune. "I hear you got a contrary fan, Ad."

"That I do, Tinker. I figure Gracie told you all about it."

"Well, you could say that, Sir, but I wasn't sure if the occasion called for 3-1 oil or holy water." Tinker chuckled as he spied the fan unplugged in the corner. "If it's okay I'll set her up on the pop cooler and take a look."

Grandad nodded as Gracie came over to Tinker, pigtails bouncing. "Ain't no she, Mr. Tinker, cause no human being I know can spit sparks, squeal like a pig and walk backwards like it can. Mr. Tinker, how can it act like it's alive and want to chase you and squeal at you and try to set you afire? And what do you plan to do with it if it comes after ya? And have you ever, in your born days, ever seen one do that?"

"Okay, Gracie, that's enough questions. Please, hush and let Tinker do his work," sighed Grandad in an apologetic way.

"It's quite alright," Tinker replied as he proceeded to work and answer Gracie at the same time.

Ten minutes later Tinker had the old fan running, its blades purring like a kitten, and mercifully blowing cool air. Granny came out and greeted Tinker and handed him a small bag of sassafras roots and a jar of honey. "Would you please tell Sadie I'll be down to visit her tomorrow and bring lunch. I figure she's pretty tuckered out by now."

"Thank you, Matilda. Yes, she was worn out some. I fixed her a cup of tea and said I'd help her to bed as soon as I got back. But she sure will enjoy a visit from you. I'll let her know, then."

Tinker decided to take a pound of fresh sausage, a pint of

peaches and a few bananas in payment for fixing the fan. "You all take care now," he said, as Gracie held the door open for him. "And Gracie, come get me if that fan starts hissing at you." Tinker laughed his way out the door. That little gal not only has a big imagination, but she asks questions even I never thought of, Tinker mused all the way home.

Grandpa's Favorite Sweet Treat
Beverly Wencek Kerr

AFTER ALICIA GRADUATED from Eastern College for Women, she returned home to teach at Zimmerton Grade School. Since she loved little children, it seemed like the best group to teach would be first grade.

At that time, salaries were not very high so, Alicia decided to stay with her parents, Clark and Evelyn Szabo, instead of buying a place of her own. Of course, they were happy to have her back home as she was their only daughter. They were proud that she had decided to make teaching her career.

Every morning Evelyn would get up and fix breakfast for Alicia and Clark before they headed to work. She had the coffee ready when they came downstairs and always had something special for them – waffles, bacon and eggs, or ham and home fries. Evelyn enjoyed cooking for her family. She had always helped her mom in the kitchen when she was just a child.

After several years and salary increases, Alicia had enough money saved to make a down payment on a house nearby. She needed to have a place of her own but didn't want to be too far from her parents in case they needed her. They were a close-knit family.

Many friends and her parents assisted Alicia with the move to her new bungalow. It didn't take long for her to feel right at home there. One day when she came home from school, she found several boxes inside her living room that definitely had not been there when she left that morning. When opening them, she discovered they were filled with books.

Her first thought was to call her mom and see if she knew

anything about the boxes of books. "Do you have any idea how these boxes of books ended up in my living room?"

Her mom calmly answered, "They were some books that I had from long ago and I thought you might enjoy reading them."

"Mom, whatever am I going to do with all these books? Where will I even put them?" wondered Alicia.

Mom smiled. "You'll be surprised what you might find in them."

Slowly, but surely, Alicia began reading the books and found she did enjoy them after a day in the classroom. She looked forward to sitting on the front porch in the swing with a glass of iced tea and a few cookies on a small table nearby. She spent time reading almost every day.

One day as she was reading, a piece of paper fell out of the book. When she opened it, she found a recipe. At the top of the paper was written, "This is Grandpa Mick's favorite candy."

Now, Alicia never met Grandpa Mick. When he came over to this country from Czechoslovakia, he worked in Lonesome Creek Coal Mine just outside of what is today Zimmerton. As with many of the coal miners, he contracted Black Lung Disease and it took his life at an early age. But her mom had talked about him many times and told how much fun they had when he wasn't working.

Since Alicia liked to try new recipes, this find really intrigued her. She ran to her parents' house and called, "Mom, you were right. I did find something interesting in one of the books today."

"What did you find? A picture? Money? Oh! Finding anything sounds exciting."

"No, Mom, it's a recipe that says it was Grandpa Mick's favorite candy."

That made Mom gasp. "Did you find the old Slovak Potato Candy recipe? I've been looking for that for years. Grandma used to make it for Grandpa every year on his birthday. I'm so glad you found it. We'll have to make some soon."

"Well Mom, it says Hunky Potato Candy."

"Hunkys were what the Slovaks that worked in the mines were called during Grandpa's time."

Alicia returned to her house and decided she would get all the things needed for the recipe at The Corner Grocery in the morning. What fun this was going to be. If it turned out well, she would even take some to school and share it with her first-grade class.

Hunky Potato Candy

- One medium sized potato
- A jigger of vanilla
- One stick of butter
- Powdered sugar
- Peanut butter

Directions:

- Peel the potato
- Boil the potato
- Mash it flat
- Add jigger of vanilla
- Blend in stick of butter
- Work in powdered sugar until no longer sticky
- Roll out dough on table covered with powdered sugar
- Cover the dough with a thick layer of peanut butter
- Roll it up carefully into a log roll
- Put it in the icebox to get hard
- Slice it
- Enjoy

Alicia didn't have any potatoes handy so, she went to The

Corner Store to see what they had. She also needed to get a big pack of powdered sugar. Then she could go home and get busy making the candy. Her mouth was watering anticipating the taste of the potato candy.

As Alicia rolled up the candy, she thought how glad she was to have an electric refrigerator rather than the ice box mentioned in her grandma's recipe. She remembered her grandma's stories of the iceman delivering large blocks of ice about a foot square to their home twice a week. With big tongs, he brought the ice from the back of his truck into the house and put it in the bottom of the icebox. It was a chore to empty the drip tray almost daily as the ice melted.

Next morning, she anxiously went to the refrigerator and sliced the candy. Even though it was breakfast time, she had to try a piece! Yum!

She quickly ran to Dad and Mom's house with samples of candy for them to try. Mom licked her lips, tasted it, and smiled. "This tastes just like the candy we used to make when I was a little girl. You did a great job of making Hunky Potato Candy."

Next stop was the first-grade classroom at Zimmerton Grade School. After lunch, Alicia said, "Last night I made some Potato Candy from a recipe my grandma used to make for Grandpa. It was his favorite candy. I brought some for you to taste today if you want to."

Candy! Of course, all the students wanted to try it. Some said, "Ew, you can't make candy out of potatoes," but they still wanted to try it.

It was a hit, and all agreed they would be happy to have some anytime she wanted to make it. Maybe Alicia would continue her grandma's tradition and make it every year for her dad's birthday, just as her grandma had made it for her grandpa's birthday...and share the candy with her students.

You never know what surprises might show up when you read an old book.

Martha's Strawberry Pie Recipe

Ingredients:
1 cup granulated sugar
1 cup water
2 Tbsp. corn starch
1 quart strawberries
1 (3 oz.) package strawberry jello

Directions:
Combine sugar, corn starch and water in a medium size sauce pan, and cook over medium heat, stirring constantly until it is the thickness of syrup. Add jello mix and stir until dissolved.

While the glaze cools, cut the strawberries into bite size pieces and gently stir them into the glaze. Then pour the mixture into your favorite pie crust, and refrigerate until ready to serve.

You can serve your pie with whipped cream, or a scoop of ice cream, but save a whole strawberry to top each slice.

And last, but not least, don't forget to add Martha's secret ingredient —

Rose
Samuel D. Besket

RETURNING HOME AND GETTING ACCLIMATED to civilian life was difficult for Justin. After a tour in Vietnam, he flinched every time he heard a thunderclap or a car backfire. Although he landed a job at a local factory, he was restless. Life wasn't the same as when he'd left. Most of his friends and girlfriends were either married or had moved away, and there wasn't much to do in his old hometown of five hundred people.

Then one day at work, Rose, a coworker, asked him if he had plans for the weekend.

"No, can't say that I do, he replied. I haven't re-entered the social scene yet."

"My niece, Shirley from San Francisco, is visiting for a few weeks. Would you like to show her around town? She's a nice girl, but, just like you, she's restless in a small town."

Before Justin could answer, Rose produced a picture of Shirley, a cute girl with short hair and a million-dollar smile.

"Sure. why not."

"Great! I'm having a cookout for the family Saturday afternoon. Why don't you stop over about three? I'm sure Shirley will be bored by then."

Just as Rose had described, she was a nice young girl studying to become a meteorologist at the University of California in Berkley. The weather for the cookout was perfect and so was Shirley. The two hit it off immediately. After some food and small talk, Justin asked if she'd like to go for a ride.

"I thought you'd never ask. This is the first time I met this side of the family. They're nice people, but I'm a little bored."

"If you don't mind getting your hair messed up, I'll put the top down on the Chevy."

"Not at all. Where are we going?" she asked, her hair blowing in the wind.

"A little town called Zimmerton. It's unique. Unlike other towns, it has maintained its originality. No box stores or strip malls. Most of the businesses are locally owned and were handed down from generation to generation. There's a wonderful town square with all the stores clustered around it. Centered in the square is a large gazebo and a century-old carousel. The crown jewel of the town is a restaurant called Martha's Place, home of the best strawberry pie west of the Ohio River. The restaurant itself is unusual. None of the tables, chairs, and silverware match."

As they topped the hill overlooking Zimmerton, they were greeted by a large sign that announced: Welcome to Zimmerton, Lucious McCallister, Mayor.

After a few hours of browsing through stores, Justin asked, "What do you think? Was I wrong about the town?"

"I'm impressed. I've never been in a store like Stylette that only sold women's clothes or Bob's Men's Store. Mom won't believe this, she only shops at Macy's. I'm glad I brought my Instamatic camera. How do you know this place so well?"

"As a child, my father lived here for ten years. His father worked at the Zimmerton Coal Company until the coal played out in the thirties. Then they moved to Guernsey County. He liked the town and brought me here often."

Looking at his watch, Justin suggested, "Why don't we take a ride on the old carousel, then go to Martha's for a piece of strawberry pie before heading home?"

Half an hour later, Shirley delicately wiped glaze from her mouth. "You're right. This is the best strawberry pie I've ever eaten. Is it a local recipe?"

"It's her grandmother's. She sold pies out the back door of

her home during the depression. Martha just took it to a new level after her grandmother passed. In real life, Martha teaches art at Zimmerton High."

As they were leaving Martha's Place Shirley sighed, "I've had so much fun today. I can't wait to tell my mom. I wish I didn't have to fly home tomorrow."

"Me, too, Shirley. Me, too. It's the first time I've really relaxed in years. I only wish you lived closer."

Except for a porch light, Rose's house was dark when they arrived home. After a hug and a kiss, Shirley said, "I'm glad Aunt Rose engineered our meeting even though it's only for one night. I'll never forget this place, or you." Squeezing his hand, she walked into the house and out of his life.

Three weeks later, Justin sat in the factory breakroom staring at his coffee. Rose and a pretty girl who Justin didn't know sat down beside him.

"Hi, Justin," Rose greeted him cheerfully. "This is Debbie. She's a new co-worker on our line. New to the factory and new to the community," she finished with a wink. "Oh," Rose said jumping up, "I forgot to clock in. See ya later."

"Hi," Justin said.

"Hi, yourself," Debbie answered.

"So, where you from?"

"Newark. I moved here to help my grandmother. She doesn't drive anymore and gets lonely."

"You live nearby?"

"No, about eight miles from here in a small town."

"How do you like living with your grandmother?"

"Great, so far. She has a house full of antiques. I love antiques, but I get bored on the weekends."

For the next week, Debbie ate lunch with Justin every day. Finally, Justin asked, "I know this is kind of sudden, but are you busy Saturday afternoon?"

"No... there's nothing I can think of. Why?"

"You like strawberry pie?"

"I love strawberries. I can eat them 'til I break out in hives." Debbie couldn't hold back a giggle.

"Well, there's a small town not far from here called Zimmerton. It's unique. Unlike other towns, it has maintained its originality. No big box stores or strip malls. Many of the businesses are locally owned and have been handed down from generation to generation. There's a wonderful town square with all the stores clustered around it. Centered in the square is a large gazebo and a century-old carousel. The crown jewel is a restaurant called Martha's Place, home of the best strawberry pie west of the Ohio River. The restaurant itself is unusual. None of the tables, chairs, or silverware match."

"Sounds like my kind of place," Debbie said. "Rose said that the white 62 Chevy in the parking lot is yours."

"It will be after twelve more payments. I'll pick you up at three."

The two hit it off beautifully and started dating. Eight months later, Justin asked Debbie to marry him.

Life opened up for Justin after he met Debbie. A few months after they were married, he was offered a job with a large automobile parts company in another town. Debbie hated to leave her grandmother and Rose, but the opportunity was too good to pass up.

One evening, months later, when Justin arrived home, Debbie told him Rose had fallen and broken her hip. "We need to visit her. It's been a while."

As they walked into her hospital room, Rose greeted them with a big smile "Well, look what the cat drug in," she said happily.

After chatting for an hour, they said their goodbyes. But on their way out, Justin stopped by the door, turned back, and asked Rose, "We have some special news, but first, do you remember that day years ago when you brought Debbie into the breakroom, then left to clock in?"

"Vaguely." Rose was getting sleepy.

"Did you forget to clock in?"

"I don't remember. But wait. You said you had special news for me. What is it?"

"Debbie is pregnant, we're going to have a little girl."

"That's wonderful." All of a sudden, Rose was awake. "Have you thought about names?"

"Yes… Rose…We're going to call her Rose."

Second Time Around
Samuel D. Besket

IT WAS ONE OF THOSE hot summer days we often get in August. Not a breeze was blowing, and the humidity was so high you could taste it.

"What a day for my truck's air conditioning to go out," Jessie thought. "Oh well, I'm only a mile from home and a cold beer." After a cool shower, Jessie sat down to enjoy his cold beer when the phone rang.

"Hello, Rose."

"Hello, Bro, got a minute to talk?"

"Does it make a difference?"

"I'm worried about Dad. Ever since Mom passed three years ago, he hardly leaves the house. He's just not interested in anything."

"I know, Rose. Every time I ask him to go fishing or play a round of golf, he turns me down. The problem is Mom and Dad were inseparable. They went everywhere together."

"I have an idea. Remember when we were kids how he used to tell us stories about Zimmerton and how grandpa used to take him there and show him around town."

"Yes, Dad took us there, too. Usually for a new pair of shoes at Karl's Shoe Store and a ride on the carousel."

"Well, Jessie. Why don't we take him there for his eightieth birthday? We could get a cake from Betsy's Bakery and have a picnic in the gazebo. Maybe it will spur his interest?"

"I'm all for it if you can get him to go. If you ask him, he will go. You and Mom could talk him into anything."

After a late-night thunderstorm, morning broke clean and

cool. Everything glistened in the morning sun and had a fresh look.

"I can't believe I let you two birds talk me into this," Justin said as he nervously squirmed in his seat. "It just doesn't seem right going there without Mom."

"Hush," Rose replied sharply. "Remember what Mom told you in the hospital? She wanted you to enjoy the time you have left, and she would save you a seat in heaven."

"Well," Justin said. "If we're going to do this, go the back way. I want to see what's left of the mine and the old house."

"Dad," Jessie interrupted. "I googled Zimmerton Coal Company. Everything has been reclaimed. The mine is a grassy hill, the houses are gone, and the railroad track is now the Great Zimmerton Trail. The main line is still there, but the trains seldom stop."

"Let's go the back way anyway, I know where the house stood."

A few minutes later, Justin said. "Stop right here. See that big rock in the creek? Dad told me he used to fish off it. The creek was a lot deeper. The railroad kept it dredged. Their house was between the creek and the railroad tracks. Every time a train passed, the house shook, and you could smell smoke and soot. If his mom had clothes on the line, she had to run out and take them down before they were covered with soot. You're right. Nothing here. I'm hungry. Let's go eat."

"I packed a lunch, Dad, just like Mom used to do. We can eat in the old gazebo."

Justin stood and gazed around the square, "Just like I said, nothing ever changes in Zimmerton. I bet the grandkids run the businesses now. Look at that sign on Judy's Flowers and Antiques. Her grandmother started that business when Dad lived here."

"What does that gizmo of yours say about Karl's Shoes and Zimmerton Tire and Magnet Shop Jessie?"

"Well, it won't be hard to find out. Let's see what Google says. Well, Karl's Shoes is owned by Karl Solomon IV, and Zimmerton Tire and Magnet Shop is still family-owned."

"What's a magnet shop?" Jessie asked with a confused look on his face.

"It was a big thing years ago. People thought magnets could cure arthritis. They wore bracelets on their wrist and around their knees. I think Karl did sell some magnets to the gypsies when they came to town."

"Did it stop the pain?"

"The only thing it stopped was people's wristwatches if they wore them on the same arm. It was a fad, just like the copper bracelets were."

"The only store that changed hands is Stylette. A Shirley Moore Bates now owns it"

"Did you say, Shirley Moore… I briefly knew a Shirley Moore years ago, but she lived in San Francisco."

"Let's see what Google knows about Shirley Moore Bates."

"Well Jessie, what does it say?"

"It says Shirley Moore was born January 13, 1946, and is a retired meteorologist From San Francisco. Married to the late Alan Bates. She has two children and recently moved to Zimmerton' Ohio."

Justin dropped his piece of chicken and stood up. "You're not joking with me are you, Jessie?"

"No. Dad, you look like you saw a ghost. Do you know this woman?"

"Rose," Justin said. "We can clean up later. Come over here. We need to talk."

"Twenty minutes later," Justin stood up. "That's the story about Shirley Moore. I still can't believe it's her. What's she doing here in Zimmerton?"

Jessie put his arm around his dad. "Want me to go check her out?"

"No, Son. She probably wouldn't remember me anyway. As I said, it was only one brief date. Besides, I'm an old man."

"Have another piece of chicken, Dad. I'll be right back."

The interior of the shop was neat and uncluttered. It resembled a picture out of a magazine.

"May I help you?" a lady with silver hair asked? "We don't get many men in here. Usually, they are towed by their wives," she said with a chuckle while offering her hand. "I'm Shirley."

"I've done my time in dress shops," Jessie responded. "But that's not the reason I'm here." Jessie paused and looked at the floor as he searched for words. "Do you know a man named Justin Von?"

Shirley dropped her pencil and slowly walked around the counter. "Why do you ask? A man named Justin Von brought me here over fifty years ago. We only met once. We did some shopping, had a piece of strawberry pie, and went home. The next day I flew back to Frisco. I never saw him again. It's funny you should mention him, I was thinking of him last week. Do you know him?"

After taking a deep breath, Jessie replied, "I'm his son."

"I've got to sit down," Shirley said as she wiped her face. "How did you find me? We never contacted each other after our first date."

"My sister Rose and I were concerned for our father after Mom passed three years ago. He seemed to lose interest in life. He loved this place. We brought him here to try to cheer him up. It was purely accidental we found you. I saw the sign in your window and googled your name."

"You have a sister named Rose? My aunt, I was visiting was named Rose."

"I know. Dad and Mom told us how she helped them get together. I guess she was the plant matchmaker."

"Wait a minute. You said you brought him here. Where is he?"

"Right across the road in the gazebo. The man wearing a Steelers ball cap."

Shirley looked out the window, then turned toward Jessie, a confused look on her face. "I would like to see him if that's possible. Does he know I'm here?"

Justin smiled, "You just might be what the doctor ordered. Yes, he knows you're here. Just like you, he was shocked to find you here."

"Excuse me a minute," Shirley said as she walked to the back of the store. A few minutes later, she reappeared minus her apron and with a fresh look on her face. "How do I look?"

"You look fine Shirley... just fine."

"Hold on to me Jessie. I can't believe this is happening. I keep looking for Alan Funt to jump out from behind a car and say, 'Smile, you're on candid camera.'"

Justin stood up as Shirley approached the gazebo. For what seemed an eternity, they stared at each other. Justin finally spoke, "I can't believe it's you. It's been a long time."

"Yes, I believe it's been almost sixty years or more. Justin, you haven't changed much. Do you still drive that 62 Chevy?"

"Unfortunately, no. If I did, I would take all of you for a ride. Why don't we sit in the shade and catch up? By the way, this is my daughter Rose."

It was obvious to Jessie and Rose the attraction was rekindled. They quietly slipped away for a coffee and donut at Betsy's Bakery.

"This is the best pastry I've ever eaten," Rose said as she reached for another one. "What is it?"

"I'm not sure. The sign said a deep-fried chocolate ice cream fritter. It's their best seller. I guess, just like everything in Zimmerton, it's an old family recipe."

"Well Bro, I have an early shift in the morning. Time to gather up Dad and head for home."

Just like their first date almost sixty years ago, Justin walked

Shirley back to her store. After a few words, she hugged him and walked into the store. Stopping by the door, she turned, "Call me, only this time don't wait so long."

Three weeks later, Rose surprised her father with an afternoon visit. "Dad, you here? It's Rose."

"Just a minute. I'm in the bedroom."

"You've been talking to Shirley, Daddy. Haven't you?"

"What makes you think that?"

"I've been trying to call you for half an hour and all I get is a busy signal."

"Look, Dad, I'm happy you found someone to spend time with. Aren't you tired of going to the movies and eating alone? Besides, I've been talking to Shirley. Just like you, she's tired of being alone. It's ok. Jessie and I are happy for you."

"We're going to meet at Martha's Place for Strawberry pie Saturday afternoon. I need new clothes. My leisure suit doesn't fit anymore. Mom always bought my clothes. I don't know where to look."

"That leisure suit belongs in a museum. Get in the car, Dad. We're going to the mall and get you back in style. Come on. Grab your wallet."

"Do you boss your husband around like this?"

"All the time. If I didn't, he'd look like you."

As they walked out the door, Jessie was walking up the sidewalk.

"Where you two going?"

"To the mall," Rose shouted as they passed. "Daddy has a date."

Harpo the Hobo
Claire Cameron

GRACIE'S DUCK, DONALD, came around the corner of the Mercantile, white wings flapping and honking like ducks usually do. Gracie felt in her apron pocket for the cracker she'd slipped in earlier and broke it in pieces for her pet. Granddaddy sat in his hand-made rocker chuckling at Gracie's spoiling Donald.

Forgetting she hadn't completed her chore she picked up the corn husk broom and went back to sweeping the steps and cement around the gas pumps. After waiting on George Hayes, Granddad went back to whittling on his newest project. Nearly finished he admired it as if that eagle was the finest work of art. Feeling as if his eyes wouldn't focus after doing the close-up work for so long, he adjusted his wire rimmed glasses. While looking up he noticed a strange figure walking up the path toward him.

"Hi there, how are you this fine afternoon?" asked the scruffy-looking man.

Gracie's eyes grew as big as the sun at high noon. Granddad turned his head squinting his eyes like he was losing his eyesight. A real live hobo, Gracie thought. The man was pitifully dressed, with patches on his shirt and holes in the toes of his shoes which were about two sizes too big. He carried a cane pole with a faded red, tattered handkerchief bag tied to it.

"Please allow me to introduce myself. My name is Harpo, and I am on a journey to see my sister, Lucille, what lives in Perry County. I'm awful hungry and I was hopin' you could spare a victual for me. I don't take handouts now, mind ya, but would play a tune or two for you in repayment." The fellow gave

Harpo the Hobo

Granddad a toothless grin as he finished his appeal for the meal. Gracie's cheeks filled with air as she tried to turn off the dank smell emanating from the hobo. Finally, she let the air out like a slowly deflating balloon. Granddad looked intently at the sorry looking soul standing in front of him and made a gesture for him to sit in the caned chair beside the steps.

"A pleasure to meet you, Sir," Granddad spoke, as he laid his eagle carving on the barrel next to him. "We don't get many musicians traveling through Zimmerton, but, have a seat. First, I'll have Gracie here, fetch you some water."

Granddad winked at Gracie, and she sped off like she'd be late for supper. Gracie was back almost as fast as she'd left carrying a pail half full of water and a chunk of soap. She smiled sweetly and set them on the stoop beside the traveler. Granddad looked embarrassed as he told Gracie what he really meant was for her to get the man a cup of cold water to drink.

"Now never you mind. The little lass was just tryin' to help. I knows I have a bit of road dust, needs washin' off."

"Well, Mr. Harpo, if you will be so kind as to give us a few minutes, Gracie and I will fetch you a bite to eat and something to wet your whistle." Harpo nodded his thanks and dipped his hands in the water. Gracie grabbed a tin cup from the cupboard and filled it with cold water as Granddad made a sandwich out of sliced bologna and cheese with a little mustard on it. On his way out the door he picked up the oatmeal cookie leftover from his mid-morning coffee break. Harpo gratefully made quick work of his "victuals," and thanked his benefactors for them.

Smacking his lips, he drew an instrument out of his raggedy bag and showed off the juice harp to his new friends. "My mammy gave this to me after my daddy died," he said solemnly. The hobo started off with a tune called *Long, Long Ago*. When that was finished, he played another. And, as Harpo continued to play, the townspeople began to gather one right after another. As he finished each song they would clap and beg for another until dusk fell on Zimmerton. An hour later the music stopped. Harpo was gifted with a piece of warm, buttered cornbread and a bowl of Granny's beans. After accepting their gracious invitation for night's lodging, Harpo fell soundly asleep on sacks full of oats in the grain store behind the mercantile. The next morning Harpo, having a full belly from breakfast, told Grandad and Granny he would like to take leave before it got too hot. Granny made up a sandwich wrapped in cheesecloth and sent along with it a juicy red apple for the road ahead. Shopkeepers and townsfolk alike, happy from their evening of entertainment and richer from meeting the happy hobo with his musical gift, came out to bid farewell to the raggedy old man as he went on to complete his dusty journey. They all waved, hands high in the air until he was out of sight and Harpo grinned his toothless grin all the way to the next town.

A to Z – Angelico to Zimmerton
Martha F. Jamail

FRANK ANGELICO WAS BORN IN the town of Bari, Italy, and later immigrated to the United States. At that time, in the early 1900's, when immigrants arrived in the country, they were often moved to places where they knew some of the people located there and could get help if needed. Frank finally settled in the community of Barre, Vermont. His friends often teased him about being placed in a town with practically the same name as his birthplace.

Frank met his future wife while he worked at a local carnival. His job at the time was to stand on a live wire and offer to shake hands with passersby. Of course, he would give them a shock as he touched them. He really enjoyed shaking the hands of the attending women, but noticed one attractive young woman who refused to shake his hand. He managed to get her name and phone number and that was the beginning of their friendship. Frank was 22 years old at the time, and the young lady, Helen, was 18. They eventually married, and their daughter, Amelia, was born on August 5, 1931.

As a child, Amelia watched her father learning how to carve and decorate granite monuments. At the time, Barre, Vermont, was the granite center of the world. Amelia remembered her father painstakingly carving the intricate roses and lilies on the surface of each monument. She loved hanging around him while he worked, but always had to maintain a safe distance. Whenever she commented about her father's artistic ability, he would grin and say, "Remember, Amelia, we Angelicos are descendants of the great Renaissance artist, Fra Angelico." She credited her own love of art to her father's talents, and her ability to cook from her talented mother. A favorite dish for all of them was the Italian pastry called gnocchi. It was savory and delicious. It was also time-consuming to prepare as with any delectable dish, so her parents would often sing and drink wine during the hours-long preparation for each dish.

When Amelia was 18 years old, she wanted to go into the nursing field. At the time, hospitals offered the only available schools for nursing education, and you had to enroll in their particular school of nursing. Amelia did her research and found that the hospital in Zimmerton, Ohio, was known for their diversity and excellent programs, so she signed up to get her training there. When one of her friends found out she was moving to Zimmerton, she laughed, teasing Amelia, "You're going to be A to Z, Amelia to Zimmerton!"

One part of the nursing program was to require participation in psychiactric training. While in that portion of training, one of Amelia's first assignments was to encourage patients to participate in group activities. At the time Amelia was a very petite 5'2" lady weighing about 115 pounds. This particular assignment was to instruct a group of patients to sing the assigned Christmas song.

After the head nurse escorted Amelia down the hall to the music room, she unlocked the door to reveal that all the patients were men who mostly were over 6 feet tall. After introducing Amelia, and giving the men their instructions to sing, the head nurse left the room, locking the door behind her. Amelia immediately panicked, intimidated by the size of the men standing around her. Glancing about the room, she noticed a nearby bench, and jumped up on it to give herself a little more height. She repeated the instructions the head nurse had given, and when the men refused to sing the Christmas carol, Amelia told them they could sing whatever they chose, but they had to sing.... And they did! They sang every verse of "One Hundred Bottles of Beer on the Wall" for an hour, and the attending nurse finally unlocked the door to release Amelia.

Amelia proved she was made of finer stuff, because even after that frightening experience, she stayed with the program. It lasted for three more months, and after that, Amelia went back to having classes and working in the nursing section of the hospital for another three months. When her term of serving in the pediatric ward ended, Amelia graduated and was hired by the hospital to work in Emergency and OR. Graduate nurses did a little of everything, and Amelia thoroughly enjoyed her time there at the hospital.

One day, she received a wedding invitation from a nurse she had befriended while in Zimmerton. Knowing it would be a good opportunity to meet many more people in the town, Amelia accepted the invitation. She always smiled thinking of going to that wedding, because that is where she met her future husband, Donald. He was the manager of the local A & P and Amelia had seen him several times while shopping there, but they had never had a chance to converse. At the wedding they found that they had a lot in common and enjoyed many of the same things. One particular thing they both enjoyed was meeting friends for dinner at Martha's Place. There was always such a welcome camaraderie there between everyone.

Actually, it was at Martha's Place that Donald had proposed. He had previously made arrangements with Martha to bring their dessert, her famous strawberry pie, with lighted candles for a unique effect. Of course, Martha was delighted to participate in such a special occasion, and stood anxiously in the background watching for Amelia's response to Donald's proposal. When Amelia happily accepted his ring, Martha and the staff cheered and applauded, joined in by the other customers who soon realized what was happening.

As time passed while Donald and Amelia enjoyed their life together in Zimmerton, Amelia began to spend more time on her artwork. Creating art was such a joy for her and a comforting reminder of the love she felt for her talented parents. She knew that Martha was also an artist, and decided one day to bring in one of her paintings to show her. In fact, Martha had sounded so pleased to see the work that Amelia brought in three different pieces – an oil painting of flowers, a watercolor of an Italian street scene, and a reverse glass painting of a bird nestled on a tree branch. Martha loved all three of them, and asked Amelia if she would like to have them displayd on the walls in the diner. Of course, Amelia immediately agreed, and Martha suggested she put an asking price on each of her paintings.

The following week, after the paintings were put on display, all three were purchased by customers who asked if there might be more available. Amelia was delighted, and graciously thanked Martha for her encouragement and assistance. When she arrived home to tell Donald the good news of the sale of her artwork, he grinned and said, "I always thought your father was right – you are a descendent of the great artist, Fra Angelico."

The Prince and the Refrigerator
Mark Cooper

"DAD," ELEANOR GREETED HER FATHER, Pete Erickson, as he answered her phone call, "I figured I'd better warn you that I told Petie about the phone pranks you pulled when you were a boy. And guess what, now he wants to try them out on you! He told me, 'Gramps is so old, he probably won't remember them.'"

"Oh, he said that, did he!?" Pete exclaimed, picturing his nine-year-old, red-headed grandson and namesake. "Does he even understand those jokes?"

"I did have to explain them," Eleanor laughed. "And I think he'd say they're a bit lame. But he also thinks it'd be fun to try to trip you up with them!"

Pete smiled as he listened to his daughter. How well he remembered the pranks he and his boyhood chums had pulled on neighbors, including making phone calls to ask those two famous questions about Prince Albert and the refrigerator. He also remembered those same neighbors' irritation at being tricked.

He especially remembered how his parents learned what he was doing. He'd called Mayor McCallister who was not known to have a good sense of humor. Unfortunately for Pete, the mayor recognized his voice and reported him to his dad. That put an end to his phone shenanigans.

With those memories running through his head, Pete assured his daughter, "Thanks for the warning, Ellie, I'll be ready!" Grinning from ear-to-ear he hung up, scheming how to have fun with his grandson.

The phone rang after dinner. Pete glanced at the caller ID. It was Petie. "Good evening. Erickson residence. How may I help you?" he answered formally.

"Um, yes sir." Petie was obviously trying to disguise his voice and sound grown up. "Mr. Erickson, can you tell me if you have Prince Albert in a can?"

"Well now," Pete answered, "Let me go check. Please hold." He laid the receiver down and counted to 15 before picking it back up. "I checked. All that's in Prince Albert's can is some chewing tobacco. I don't see him. He must have left!"

"Oh, well, uh…" Obviously Petie had not been prepared for his grandpa's answer. "That's good, I guess."

"Will that be all?" Pete questioned.

"Oh yeah, is your refrigerator running?"

"Not on your life!" Pete responded. "I never let it run. Its sitting in the corner of the kitchen right where it belongs." The phone line fell silent as Pete held in his laughter.

Finally, his grandson spoke, now in his normal voice. "Oh Gramps. You're no fun! That's NOT what you're supposed to say!"

"Oh yeah?" Pete retorted, "I may be an old man, but I can still think fast, just like when I was a red-headed kid like you!" Then he chuckled, "Tell you what Petie. I've got to go into Zimmerton for a haircut tomorrow. Why don't you call Grandma then and ask her about Prince Albert and the refrigerator. I bet you'll be able to fool her with those jokes." Petie giggled. "Thanks Grandpa. I'll let you know what she says."

After hanging up the phone, Pete turned to his wife who was just shaking her head at him. "Honey, Petie's going to call you in the morning with those Prince Albert in the can and refrigerator running jokes. Promise you'll play along?"

She smirked, "Maybe I will. Maybe I won't. I can't let you have all the fun!"

* * *

The Prince and the Refrigerator

JUST IN CASE YOU ARE NOT familiar with these vintage jokes that Petie and Grandpa were sharing, here's how they are supposed to go.

> Do you have Prince Albert [chewing tobacco] in a can?
> Well, yes, I do.
> Then why don't you let him out?

> Is your refrigerator running?
> Yes, it is.
> You'd better stop it before it runs away!

Shenanigans
Claire Cameron

FOUNDERS DAY WAS HELD ON the Fourth of July week-end and, that Saturday, the Fitzgerald twins would celebrate their sixteenth birthdays. Both girls had begged and pleaded for their father to allow them to work in the kissing booth to raise money for the Founder's Scholarship Fund. But after considering the girls' previous shenanigans, Reverend Fitz's first and second answer was a firm "no!" However, after much urging from the mayor's wife, Rachel, Reverend Fitz agreed to allow them to spend two hours there as long as Rachel would oversee them and set a time limit and rules for kissing. Kisses weren't cheap, but it was worth every penny to the young fellows who had eyes on their favorite girl. Two kisses for a dollar. No open mouth kissing nor lingering more than thirty seconds on each kiss.

The booths, the signs and as many other preparations as possible had been completed by Thursday afternoon. Then before the official opening on Friday the ladies set up the tables, warmed food, had beverages prepared, and made sure local musicians were ready to start playing live music. The Modern Woodsman Hall sat on the east corner of the baseball field and was decked out in soft light inside and out. Bales of straw and benches gave dancers a place to rest their weary feet while red and white checked covered tables served as places to set punch, popcorn, and donuts.

Saturday's schedule was tight, but workable as vendors and workers stocked and arranged their colorful and eye-catching displays for the 8:00 am opening. So, while some browsed and made purchases, others strolled around leisurely, munching kettle-cooked corn or donuts, sipping lemonade, or the homemade draft root beer Zimmerton was famous for. The young crowd enjoyed the dunking machine and the kissing booth. Those of a more mature age took in the flea and farmer's markets, where creative folks were crafting jewelry, leather goods, brooms, and a variety of other handmade items. The booths and the markets would shut down during the parade since everyone would be watching it.

Zimmerton's mayor, Lucious McAllistar, finished applying the finishing touches to his 1958 Chevy Corvette. With Lucious being the Grand Marshal this fine automobile, his pride and joy, would lead the parade. His son, Lucious the III, better known as Mac, beamed as his father patted his shoulder, handing him the clean floor mats. "I left you the easy job of placing these floor mats back inside. Are you sure you will have the signs made up and attached to this fine specimen before the parade begins, son?"

"You can count on me, father. The signs are ready for me to put on now."

"Excellent!" said the mayor. "Now please have the car in the first position in front of the town square by 3:00. The rest of the vehicles will line up in order behind it. I'd like you and your mama ready to ride with me with wide smiles and plenty of hand waving. Your mama has a jar of suckers ready to toss to the children and your job will be to throw out badges that say, "***Re-elect Mayor McAllister.***"

Mac gave his father a nod of affirmation as he walked around the Corvette admiring it. Unbeknownst to his father, he dreamed about cruising around the block in it with pretty little Hope Fitzgerald by his side.

Faith and Hope had just returned from Carlisle's Mercantile with their new hair ribbons and the coconut their mother Caroline needed to top the cream pies. Six delectable coconut cream pies were nearly ready for the pie eating contest.

"Now girls I'm counting on you to deliver these pies to the pie cooler for the contest. Martha and Betsy will be there to watch over them and have them ready for the contestants." Betsy was Martha's primary baker and trusted assistant, famous for her homemade fresh strawberry pies. "As soon as we get our ribbons tied in our hair, Hope and I will take the pies down. Then we thought we might get a root beer and popcorn before we have to be at the kissing booth," Faith said smiling.

The girls' mother, Caroline, looked up tilting her head to the side with a vague feeling of apprehension coming upon her. Therefore, she answered swiftly remembering their previous mischievous antics. "Your father will have eyes on both of you and may show up when you least expect it so take heed and mind your manners. Remember you represent the family of God and His church."

"Yes, Mama," both girls said sweetly. A few minutes later the girls were walking down the sidewalk pies in hand smiling as if carrying a well-hidden secret.

Martha and Betsy greeted and thanked the girls while each commented on who might win the pie eating contest. The girls noticed the table and chairs in front of the bleachers with a seat for each one of the judges, Mayor McAllister, Martha from Martha's Place and Chief of Police, Harvey Hamilton. The judges would determine who had the heartiest appetite in Zimmerton. The contestants' table was set with napkins, spoons, and glasses to be filled with milk, generously donated by Broughton's Dairy. Various fruit and cream pies were donated by Zimmerton's most famous bakers including Betsy, Caroline Fitzgerald, and Birdie Williams. First, second and third place prizes would be given by Martha's Place. Each prize consisted of special coupons for Martha's Place where the food was delicious and the atmosphere warm and inviting.

Leaving the pies in good hands Faith and Hope moved on to partake of fresh popped corn and root beer. As they walked the well-worn path of the ball diamond, Papa's words echoed in Faith's mind. "I'll be watching you girls in the kissing booth so I trust you will behave like proper young ladies. Mrs. McAllister will give me a full report, too. She is in charge so, remember the rules."

Just then Hope nudged Faith's arm noticing her thoughts were far away. "What?" questioned Faith, irritated at the interruption.

Hope was quick to reply. "Remember, I will say I have to go fetch something from home and will be gone a bit and then I'll take over for you when I get back."

"I know, Hope! I also know when it will be your turn to be me so I can go swimming with Barlo and his sister."

Hope saluted with her free hand. If anything goes wrong, we won't be lying when asked, since you'll be me and I'll be you. "Hope's mouth turned upward in a sly smile. "I can't wait to see Mac and take a ride in his daddy's car!"

Ignoring Hope's last comment, Faith sighed wondering how many boys she'd get to kiss today. A smile finally replaced the pout that had been on her lips as she thought about the shenanigans that she and her sister planned to enjoy this weekend.

After checking on his daughters in the kissing booth, Reverend Fitz was first on the dunking machine, then Doc Adams followed. Both got knocked off into the cold water on the third pitch of the ball. The middle school gang had been laughing, joking, and shouting at the poor souls sitting on the stool waiting apprehensively anticipating the shock of the cold water. Birdy Williams was beginning to regret agreeing to this, but Cora Phelps, President of the Order of the Purple Hat Society, had tempted her by offering to buy her tickets to the dinner theater next weekend. "Besides," Cora told her sweetly, "this is for a good cause." Birdie shivered and her face went pale thinking what a sight she must be in her bright red bathing cap and purple bathing suit, which seemed to have shrunk since last summer.

"Hey Birdie, tweet, tweet, tweet! You'd better fly on outa

there 'fore ya get all wet!" Hollered red headed Petie Erickson.

"Yeah, Birdie, you'd better go before ya sink!" yelled another. Just at that time, perklunk! Birdy hit the water and the impact sent water spewing through the crowd.

"Ahhahahahaha!" The boys were laughing so hard they couldn't catch their breath! Petie yelled, "Someone better call the fire department. It'll take a whole tank to refill the dunker since Birdie...ugh, oh...!" His voice trailed off as his father's huge hand covered the boy's mouth. Petie's buddies, their eyes bigger than fifty cent pieces, scattered as fast as their feet could carry them for fear they would be next to feel Mr. Erickson's wrath.

Cora handed Birdie a towel and dabbed the tears from her eyes as she leaned on her friend. "There, there, Birdie, let's get you changed, go over to the Auxiliary Hall and have a nice cup of hot tea." Cora spoke sympathetically. By the time the tank was refilled, Karl, owner of Karl's Shoes, was sitting on his perch making faces and daring anyone to "drop" him.

Across the way, faces were smeared with pie as the pie eating contest was in full swing. Honk Touvell, the favored contestant, was ahead by half a pie, but Sissy Marling was close behind. Moonie Baker and the school janitor, Joey Jenkins, were also putting pie away very quickly. The lightweight contestants were halfway through or just finishing their first pie. Fans of all ages were rooting for their favorite pie lover. So far, the fresh strawberry pie which Martha had made was the favorite with coconut cream running a close second. The judges were busy taking notes and tallying scores.

Hope, who had earlier accepted the chance to take a short ride around town with Mac, was smiling eagerly as she sat by his side. Her admirer started the newly polished car and eased it onto the street and around the town square. "Hope, would you consider sitting with me at the picnic lunch tomorrow? I really like you and how your eyes sparkle. Or maybe you'd like to go with me to a movie sometime?" Mac asked hopefully.

"I'd love to, Mac, but Papa made it clear, no dating yet. I'm taking a chance being here with you now," Hope replied, eyes downcast.

"Well, don't be sad. Let's enjoy the ride and talk about it later."

"That sounds good to me," whispered Hope.

Mac had just taken his eyes off the road a moment when splat! A bird hit the windshield causing him to swerve to the right onto the alley between the judges and the pie eating table. Blinded by the sun and panicked, the boy didn't react quickly enough.

Before he could hit the brakes, Hope yelled "Mac, look out!" But it was too late. The right front tire clipped the left corner of the pie table tipping it up, sending pies airborne. A Dutch apple pie sailed right over Caroline's head. She had just set another strawberry pie in front of Joey Jenkins when it flew west and hit the mayor right between the eyes.

The car continued veering down the alley. A heavy rain the night before had left a huge muddy hole in the middle of the alley, which most everyone had been successful in avoiding. Everyone except young Mac and Hope. The boy slammed his foot on the brake just a couple seconds before the car slid and sank bumper-deep into the mud hole. By that time fruit pies, cream pies, and mud pies had landed on faces, heads and in the laps of startled watchers. And young Mac and Hope Fitzgerald were in a heap of trouble. It was a sight for sore eyes. No one moved for nearly five minutes as if the judges and spectators were all in a trance. And the two occupants of the most prized car in Zimmerton hung their heads in shame.

At 3:15 the voice of Councilman Barry Thomas came alive over the loudspeaker. "Zimmerton would like to thank everyone for coming out to celebrate Founders Day. I'm sorry to announce that due to circumstances beyond our control the parade is being rescheduled for tomorrow at 3:00. At that time winners of today's contests will be announced. Church services and the box luncheon will go on as previously scheduled. Thank you for your understanding. Enjoy the music and kick up your heels to the Frontier Brothers Band performing at 7:00 tonight in the Modern Woodman Hall."

On Sunday morning, Petie Erickson was red faced and stuttering as he stood before the church congregation and gave a heartfelt apology to Birdie for his shameful behavior the day before.

After church the twins sat fretting in their room since their conspiracy to pass Hope off as Faith had landed them the humiliation of being grounded while everyone else continued celebrating the remainder of Founders Day. Since their parents, one step ahead of them, had marked the twins' initials inside their purses, they were caught red-handed.

Much to the Mayor's relief Pop's eldest son of Pop's Garage, had the mayor's car looking good as new as it took its place in the Founder's Day Parade.

And can you believe it, thanks to Mac and Hope's accident, Sissy Marling was announced winner of the pie eating contest. Besides the four pies that she had already eaten in front of her, she had eaten the three pies that had landed upside down right next to her, while the other contestants sat gaping at Mac, Hope and the Mayor's muddy car. Although Faith and Hope's plans for misbehavior brought them a world of trouble, their shenanigans made Sissy's day.

Bonnie's Gypsy Spirit Lives On
Beverly Wencek Kerr

BONNIE ALWAYS BOUGHT A LOTTERY TICKET each week as she knew it was her only possibility of being able to become a gypsy. Everyone told her she was wasting her money, but Bonnie had to try. Then, she stopped at The Mercantile to check the winning numbers. This week, she looked carefully at her numbers and compared them to the winning numbers.

7, 12, 21 She had them all! Her hands shook as she continued checking. 30, 41 She had both of those too. One more to go! Could this really be happening? The last number was 45. Again. Bonnie checked all the numbers. She had them all! "I won! I won!" Bonnie jumped up and down and even did a little dance.

She ran out the door and down to Martha's to tell the good news. Everyone cheered and clapped. No one in Zimmerton had ever won the big lottery before. When things settled down a little, Martha said, "Strawberry pie for everyone to celebrate this happy occasion."

As the customers ate their pie, her friend Judy expressed the feelings of all, "Bonnie, you've worked so hard all your life. You deserve something special."

This was her chance to fulfill her lifelong dream. Travel! Travel wherever the road happened to lead. All her life she had tried to save enough money to be free to travel the United States, and now she had her opportunity.

Bonnie's dream of travel had begun years earlier while growing up on a farm just outside Zimmerton. She'd been ten years old when the gypsies camped there. Back then, she had said, "Someday I am going to be a gypsy." Now it was time to leave the farm, where she still lived with her brother Frank, and live her dream adventure.

Years before winning the lottery, while in high school, Bonnie worked at Martha's Place as a waitress. Later, she became the manager while Martha was busy teaching art at Zimmerton High School. Customers enjoyed having Bonnie around as she always dressed in the brightest clothes with long flowing skirts and sparkling jewelry.

Customers also liked her advice for aches and pains and her premonitions about things that were going to happen. Judy sat down for a cup of tea and told Bonnie, "My head hurts so bad. I have these headaches every once in a while. Any suggestions?"

"Well, Judy, why don't you try some peppermint oil? Put a drop on each temple and on the inside of each wrist. Then rub your finger under your nose. Wait for 15 minutes and see if you don't feel better."

"I'll give that a try as the doctor just wants to give me pain pills." Judy went to the Mercantile to find some pure peppermint oil.

Sometimes Bonnie would just have a strong feeling about something. One day when Adam stopped for pie and coffee before heading to get some new items for his store, The Mercantile, Bonnie suddenly felt the urge to tell him, "Watch out for deer along the way. Don't want you to have an accident."

Adam smiled but did keep his eyes open for deer as he traveled down the road. Sure enough one popped out when least expected, but since Adam had been watching carefully, he avoided hitting it. That Bonnie was right again, he thought. She always seems to know when something is going to happen.

Another day Shirley came in complaining of her arthritis. "My joints ache so much that I can hardly hold onto a cup of coffee. What should I do?"

"The best thing I know is to go to Zimmerton's Tire and Copper and get one of his copper bracelets. They work like magic."

Shirley actually left her piece of strawberry pie on the table and hurried down the street to get that copper bracelet. "I'll let you know if it works."

Once Mayor Lucious came into Martha's and bragged, "I bought a new 1971 Chevy Vega!"

Bonnie shook her head, "That car is going to cause you problems."

Shaking his finger, Lucious assured her, "The 1971 Chevy Vega has just been named the Motor Car Trend of the Year. It's going to be great."

It wasn't long before Lucious found his new car was leaking oil. Days later his gas tank caught on fire. Guess Bonnie was right again.

While the smoke was still settling from the mayor's unfortunate Vega, Bonnie was thinking about what kind of vehicle she would need. She had fond memories of the Gypsy Wagon that camped on their farm long ago. That wagon with its bright colors and designs had been the gypsies' home while they traveled. That was the kind of life she wanted. Before you know it, Bonnie had purchased a small motor home and had Martha use her art skills to brighten it with some colorful designs.

Bonnie always had that entrepreneur blood flowing through her veins so she tried to think of a business she could take with her in her travels. It wasn't that she really needed the money since she had won quite a nice sum from the lottery. Her wish was to do something that would give others enjoyment and make them feel good. So, she began looking for that special dream job. Besides pondering this herself, she asked the customers, "What can I sell along the way?"

Ralph gave his opinion, "You might sell copper bracelets in your travels since they really helped my wife Shirley with her arthritis. Don't forget, somehow you always seem to know what is going to happen. Maybe you should tell fortunes like the gypsies."

Judy weighed in, "Whatever else you do, sell oils. My headaches went away quickly when I used the peppermint oil you recommended.".

Thus, began Mystical Bonnie's adventures throughout the United States. It wasn't long before she was not only selling her oils and copper bracelets but also telling people's fortunes just like she remembered the gypsy Naomi doing in the camp so many years ago.

Having everything she needed in her small camper, travel was easy and enjoyable. Seeing her colorful wagon with Mystical Bonnie written on the side, people at a campground where she stayed would gather around her to ask either for some advice to help ease their aches and pains, or perhaps to look into their future.

At one camp, she met a couple who were headed to Lily Dale in New York. Lily Dale was a Spiritualist settlement centered around beliefs in God, Jesus, and the Bible as well as the religion of continuous life. Residents of the settlement sold oils and did readings for people. Bonnie's new friends thought she would enjoy being with other people who shared her interests.

That fascinated Bonnie and before you know it, she was headed to Lily Dale to see what she might learn. Once there, she stayed at the Maplewood Hotel and enjoyed evenings sitting on the porch listening and learning. Many there realized that Bonnie had an unusual gift for seeing into the future and they began listening to her instead of her listening to them. Spirits were often felt in the hotel, and you might hear a guest run out the door shouting, "Someone's in the hall, I hear them walking but can't see anyone."

Set on the shores of Cassandra Lake, Lily Dale's peacefulness attracted visitors throughout the summer months. The connection to nature led Bonnie to walk the forest trail to Inspiration Stump where messages were given by mediums. Bonnie watched the ceremony as one person after another received a message about their life. I could do that, thought Bonnie.

While Bonnie was not formally permitted to give messages until she had proper training and approval, she continued to tell people what she saw in their future. It was her favorite way to spend her evenings on the hotel's front porch.

One evening Bonnie ventured into the Indian sweat lodge there. Once inside, the door was closed, and everyone was smudged with sweet grass, sage, or cedar for cleansing and purification. "My loose dress was soaked after the heat and scents purified my body," she told Anna that evening as they sat on the front porch. "I do feel better now."

Someone told Bonnie that in the winter, many people went to another Spiritualist camp in Cassadaga, Florida. So, when September rolled around, Bonnie headed that way, making many stops at campgrounds along the way.

When she arrived in Cassadaga, she discovered it had been named "The Psychic Capital of the World." Here she was introduced to the world of healing. This camp had a hotel, auditorium, library, cottages, and a temple surrounded by sunflowers. This will be my winter home, thought Bonnie.

One day as she was walking to the auditorium, she stopped to talk to a visitor. "Hello," greeted Bonnie. "I'm so glad you came to visit us today. My name is Bonnie and I'm learning about natural healing. I've been experimenting with oils ever since we had a gypsy wagon camp on our farm years ago."

"Did you say Bonnie? Would that be Bonnie Byers? I'm Miri. Remember how we used to walk and talk about things to cure?"

"Oh, Miri," Bonnie cried, "I can't believe we've found each other after all these years. Yes, I'm Bonnie Byers. See that camper over there that says Mystical Bonnie – that's me! We have a lot of catching up to do."

After that, Bonnie and Miri frequently traveled together around the country telling fortunes, selling oils, and healing people by natural means. Sometimes Bonnie could tell what was wrong with a person just by talking to them. They both enjoyed the friendly, peaceful atmosphere at the Spiritualist camps.

Once in a while, Bonnie even made a side trip to Zimmerton to see her brother Frank, who still lived on their old farm. Of course, she always stopped in at Martha's for some of her strawberry pie. There she told everyone, "Remember when I said for years that someday I was going to be a gypsy? Well, 'someday' finally happened!"

Stuff That Happens at Stan's Station
Mark Cooper

ZEDEKIAH WASN'T THE BRIGHTEST BULB in the socket nor the sharpest arrow in the quiver. Stanley Shepard had known that before hiring him to do odd jobs at his station. But Zedekiah's never-met-a-stranger personality made him one of the most likable characters in Zimmerton. His eccentricities were more than made up for by the friendly atmosphere he helped create in the store.

Stan gave Zedekiah the responsibility of stocking shelves. Chips and candy with the quickest approaching "best used by" dates needed to be placed at the front of the shelves and display racks. After several weeks, Zedekiah was proud to have finally grasped the concept.

In the back room, Stan had a safe filled with several hundred dollars worth of rolled coins. Every morning he took the coins he'd need for that day's change and deposited them in the register. His employees were 100% trustworthy so he didn't worry about the fact that the safe's lock no longer worked.

Imagine his shock the day he found Zedekiah sitting in the back room, safe open, and ALL the coins, thousands of them, out of their individual wrappers and piled high on a table.

"Zedekiah!!! What the ... heck are you doing?!" Stan cried, picturing the hours it would take to resort and re-roll the coins.

"Mr. Shepard! These here coins was all out of order and mixed up. I mean, just in one roll of quarters, some were dated two years ago, and some were 50 years old. I'm sorting them all by their date, so's you can get the oldest ones used up first just like we do with the candy and chips. Mr. Shepard, I can't believe no one else here has realized this needed doin'!"

"Well Zedekiah," Stan said after taking a deep breath and counting to ten, "You are right; no one else has EVER thought about sorting the coins so we use the oldest first. Carry on." He walked back out front to the register, shaking his head and thinking, It's high time I get the lock on that safe fixed.

...

"Mr. Shepard, I'm sorry about the condition of my money," Clyde said as he handed crumpled five- and ten-dollar bills across the counter. "I was repairing the awning at Martha's. Just as she paid me, it cut loose and poured down rain. I needed to get my tools put away fast, so I stuffed the money in my pocket and now it's a mess."

"No worries, Clyde," Stan replied, "When people pay me with wrinkled and torn money, it goes in a special compartment in the register. Then when I have a rude customer, I use it to pay back their change. I do it with a smile and a 'thank you,' but am also getting even with them for being rude."

Clyde threw his head back and laughed. "Payback – that's a funny one. You're paying back their change and their bad behavior at the same time. That's being really smart with your money!"

...

Elsie rolled her eyes. Yet another customer was talking on his cell phone while she was trying to ring up his purchases, "Is there anything else for you?" The customer ignored her and kept talking. Elsie hit the total button. "That'll be $13.76 please."

"Oh, I need cigarettes. Marlboro's."

Elsie clicked out of the payment screen and scanned in the Marlboro's. "OK, I got them. Anything else?" The customer had gone back to talking on the phone. Elsie hit the total button again.

"Wait, wait, wait!" The customer said abruptly. "I need to grab a can of pop!"

"Go ahead," Elsie's patience was reaching its breaking point. She was tired of customers talking on their cell phones while she was trying to help them complete their transactions.

The customer put the pop on the counter and asked impatiently, "WELL, how much is it?" He jammed his credit card into the card reader. Elsie had had enough. She quietly hit the cancel button on her register. "Declined" popped up on the payment screen. Hiding her smirk, Elsie spoke loudly so that all those waiting in line could hear, "I'm so sorry sir, but your credit card has been declined! Please step aside so I can help all these other folks behind you."

The customer went slinking out the door, embarrassed that everyone had heard that his credit card was declined. He was also stressed, wondering why it had been declined.

On the other hand, Elsie felt vindicated. Once in a while, getting revenge on a rude customer was well-worth losing a sale.

...

"I need to pee, then I'm going to buy some stuff!" the woman gushed as she sailed in through the door.

Elsie turned to Mr. Shepard, "Why do people feel the need to tell us that not only are they going to the bathroom, but also describe what they are going to do once they get in there?"

Stan shook his head. "Beats me. At least she said she is planning to buy something. It irks me when people come to in to use the bathroom, but don't have the courtesy to buy a candy bar or something to help pay for the paper, water, and soap they use."

Elsie signed, "You're assuming they actually USE the soap."

...

Every day Stan writes a thought-provoking or amusing quote on the dry erase board hanging behind the counter. Customers enjoy discussing the wit and wisdom they read there. This is what I read this morning when I stopped in for my cup of coffee,

"If it ain't fixed, why bother break'n it?" – Zedekiah

Discovering Zimmerton for Christmas

Mark Cooper

"OH, COME ON HON," Mike urged, "this will be fun!" Jody, his pretty bride, wasn't convinced. When they'd moved back to Mike's home community near Zimmerton, he'd promised that in December they'd splurge and take a weekend to visit the city where she'd grown up. They would stay at the ritzy Clairemount House, attend City University's Christmas Concert, shop in the exclusive Eddington's Department Store, and dine at the high-class City View Restaurant with its linen napkins and snooty maître-d.

Jody had studied at City University. So had Mike. When they met, she thought his country simplicity was cute. He'd been in awe of her city sophistication. She'd made it clear that she wanted to continue living in a metropolitan area after their marriage. He'd agreed, even though secretly he longed for the country. His love for Jody made living in the city seem a small sacrifice.

Their plans had turned upside down after their August wedding. The very day they returned from their honeymoon Mike received an email from his Uncle Joe.

Mike, your granddad has decided to retire. His decision took us all by surprise. I'm going to cut to the chase. We desperately need someone who is young, energetic and understands business finance to help run this place. As you have probably heard, the company is growing, and we've got to get ourselves computerized and all that to stay competitive and up-to-date. You interested?

The moment Mike shared the email with Jody, she knew

they'd be moving. She had heard his wonderful memories of working in the family business when he was growing up. His family pride ran deep, and he'd like nothing more than to become part of their business. So, in spite of her qualms, she'd urged him to take the job, telling herself she would adjust to country life.

The little farmhouse they moved into sat on Uncle Joe's farm, just a few miles from Zimmerton. "Don't worry about paying rent!" Uncle Joe assured them. "You get the place cleaned up and just enjoy it!" Jody enjoyed making the house comfortable and homey. Dated wallpaper was torn off the walls, cracked plaster got patched, and dark, 1970s era, paneling received fresh coats of cheerful paint. Mike's Aunt Rose helped her select material from the local "you-can-buy-anything-here" mercantile and taught her how to sew new curtains for the windows. The antique farm table and ladder-back chairs in the kitchen, a corner cupboard in the dining room, and a huge roll top desk in the living room had come with the place. After a careful cleaning and polishing, their mellowed woodwork gleamed and added to the cozy atmosphere of the home.

All of that seemed of little value to Jody right now. Even the Christmas tree they'd decorated after cutting it themselves on Grandpa's farm looked dejected. Jody was so disappointed that they were having to cancel their special weekend in the city. But she accepted there was no other choice, given the major winter storm that had shut down the upper half of the state, including the city.

Their own local roads were treacherous, but still drivable. That was why Mike suggested they spend the day in Zimmerton, in place of going to the city.

"Oh, come on hon! This will be fun!" he insisted. Jody didn't see how a day in Zimmerton could compare to any of their ruined plans for a weekend in the city. But she also knew Mike was trying to cheer her up.

"OK, let's do it," she agreed, trying to smile.

They bundled themselves into insulated jeans, heavy sweaters and coats, and awkward looking boots, their country get-up a far cry from the new gown she'd bought for the concert, and the suit she'd secretly purchased for Mike.

The four-wheel drive pickup cut through the snow-covered roads. Jody would have almost welcomed their sliding into a ditch, just to spare her from Zimmerton. But no such luck. As they drove along the hilltop road above the valley, she noticed Mike was slowing down. Surely, he couldn't be thinking about turning onto.... oh no, his turn signal was on.... he WAS!

"Mike, what are you thinking?" Jody screeched, "Don't you dare take Bossy's Hill!"

Mike laughed, "It's a short cut!"

"Yeah, a short cut to the cemetery!"

With its steep slope, hairpin turns, and numerous blind spots, Bossy's Hill was dangerous in good weather. Most locals considered it absolute tomfoolery to attempt it in bad conditions.

As they started down the hill, the first 90-degree bend approached quickly. "Mike, slow down!" Jody begged. The truck slid just a little going into the turn, but Mike kept control of the wheel. Jody breathed a sigh of relief, only to see the next curve approaching, this one a 180-degree bend. Old Timers maintained that Old Bossy, the cow credited with cutting the first path down the hill that eventually became a road, must have had a fly in her ear when she created this curve.

"Mike," Jody plead, "you've got to slow down!!"

"Can't sweety. If I try to use the break, we'll slide." Jody covered her face and shut her eyes in terror and waited for the end. It didn't come. Indeed, when she peeked, they were safely past the curve and heading towards the next one. She thought of the roller coasters she used to enjoy at the City Amusement Park back home. This is just a little bit fun. She kept her eyes open and admired how her husband wrestled the truck around the bend and down the final straight stretch into the valley. From there it was smooth sailing after they turned on to the state route and drove up the opposite hill into Zimmerton.

Mike parked on a side street that was still covered with several inches of snow. "Where to first?" he asked.

"This is your town. You lead the way!" Jody responded.

"You wanted a unique gift for your dad, right? Any ideas yet?"

Jody shook her head no. "What do you think?" she asked.

"Well, he likes desserts. Let's go to Martha's Place. She has the best homemade pies. Buy a frozen one and Martha's will mail it to him."

The moment they stepped into the shop, Jody grabbed Mike's arm. "I can't believe it, that sign says they have elderberry pie. Dad talked about his grandma making it when he was a boy. He hasn't had one for decades!"

Their pie order completed, the young couple crossed the street to The Corner Grocery. An old-fashioned bell hanging over the door jangled, announcing their arrival. Mike led Jody to a section just left of the front door, "The 'Corner' has this special section of foods, all made by local cooks."

Jody was surprised at the vast array of jellies, jams, salsa, and BBQ sauces. "Uncle Martin likes trying unusual foods. I'll think I'll get him this jar of quince and pear salsa."

Back outside her attention was caught by a quaint sign hanging over the sidewalk, Judy's Flowers and Antiques. "Oh, let's go in here!" she said eagerly. Mike grinned. He was thrilled to see his wife warming up to Zimmerton. Inside the store their eyes were drawn to a large display that featured neither antiques nor flowers. They both gasped at the array of hand-crafted wooden toy trains, cars, trucks, and farm equipment.

Judy noticed their interest and came over, "These are all made by Harold Greene. Once he retired, his wife threatened to leave him unless he found some reason to get out of her way and out of the house. He took up woodworking. She says he should have taken it up years ago. He makes more selling his stuff here and online than he ever did working at the Stone Quarry!"

Mike picked up a truck and turned it over, "Look, he's signed his work. I think I'll get this for my nephew." Jody noticed him also looking with longing at a highly detailed replica of an old Ford truck. "That looks like the truck my Granddad had. He let me sit in his lap and steer it when I was just 5 years old." She made a mental note to return to the store on her own. That truck would make a wonderful gift for Mike. He'd be so surprised.

"Cold?" Mike asked as they stepped back outside. He put his arm around Jody and pulled her close while steering her around the corner towards the Zimmerton Volunteer Fire Department. The original fire truck, retired from active service, sat out front with its single red light slowly revolving. A huge wreath hung off the hood ornament. Inside the simple cement-block building, white plastic folding tables held crock pots of sloppy joe while hot dogs and hamburgers waited in warmers. "Hungry?" Mike asked.

"Sure," Jody answered, surprised at how wonderful the hot food smelled. Then she saw dozens of donuts, also homemade. Steaming coffee and hot chocolate added their aroma. Jody was stunned when she saw the sign next to the food, "Cost by Donation." You'd never see that in the city, she mused to herself.

They sat on folding chairs around a card table near the window. "The Lady's Auxiliaries for the fire department and the hospital work together to put this on every Saturday in December. They split the money to help buy new equipment for both the fire department and the hospital," Mike explained. "This year the fire department will finally have enough money to buy a new pumper. Well, not new-new, but new to Zimmerton!"

Warmed by the hot food and with Styrofoam cups of steaming coffee in hand, the couple went back outside and strolled along the sidewalk. By now Jody was enjoying the simplicity of the village's Christmas scenery. Greenery and red bows wrapped every old-fashioned looking streetlamp. Multi-colored lights lit shop windows. Stately buildings and homes looked elegant with single candles glowing in each window. Best of all, the good citizens of Zimmerton greeted friends and strangers alike as they passed by. Jody had to admit that this village's Christmas setting was much more peaceful and relaxing than anything they would have experienced in the city.

Thanks to the clouds, dusk fell early. Mike and Jody trudged back to the truck through the evening shadows. After stowing their packages in the cab, Mike turned to Jody, "One more stop," he said.

Taking her hand, he led her towards the gazebo on the village square. She hadn't paid attention to it earlier in the day. But now it and the snow-kissed evergreens on the square glowed with thousands of tiny white lights. In the shelter of the gazebo, parishioners from local churches were performing a living nativity.

As the young couple stood silently and drank in the peaceful scene, members of Zimmerton's church choirs moved into place and began to sing.

"Joy to the world, the Lord is come..."

Jody snuggled closer to her husband's side. True, these volunteer singers were no match for the City University Chorale, but still, they sounded pretty nice.

A group of white-robed children stood on a low platform behind the gazebo. Their voices rang out pure and clear.

"Hark! The herald angels sing, 'Glory to the newborn King.'"

Jody noticed Mike quickly brushing his eyes, "Maybe someday we'll have a kid up there."

The young woman portraying Mary picked up the doll representing the Christ Child. The choir sang softly, no instrumental music accompanying them.

"Silent Night, Holy Night. All is Calm. All is Bright...."

Whether by design or by accident, an interior light in a nearby church came on, shining through its stained-glass cross. The glow of the cross illuminated the snow all the way to the gazebo and the living nativity.

"*O holy night! The stars are brightly shining. It is the night of the dear Savior's birth....*"

"Mike," Jody whispered. She could say no more as tears streamed down her face. She had never imagined that in tiny Zimmerton she would come face to face with such a stunning display of the ancient, yet up-to-date, Christmas message.

As the two of them walked back to the truck they simultaneously reached for each other's hand and intertwined their fingers. "Isn't this perfect?" Mike murmured in her ear.

"Yes," Jody answered softly. Then, in a firmer tone, she added, "Well, almost perfect. It will be completely perfect if you do not take Bossy's Hill on the way home!"

Family

Betsy Taylor

"OH! GOOD HEAVENS!"

Ten-year-old Marley Davis turned toward the woman whose outburst had startled her as she poured over a rack of birthday cards. The woman stared at Marley as if she'd seen a ghost.

"Are you okay?" Marley feared the woman might be having a heart attack. With her palm pressed to her chest, she certainly looked like she might collapse at any moment.

"I – I'm okay. But . . ." The woman stammered that Marley was the image of someone she'd known a long time ago. She finished by saying, "Pay me no mind. It was a foolish notion."

"Who was it? The person you knew," Marley asked as she helped the woman sit on a nearby bench.

The woman shook her head to clear it. "She was my niece."

"Was?"

"We lost her when she was nearly two."

"I'm so sorry." Marley offered to bring her a bottle of water. But the woman, who said her name was Dora, refused.

"Really, don't worry about me. I was just startled by your resemblance to my niece. It's the hair color. Very unusual."

Marley stiffened. Her hair color had been remarked upon all her life. The red, gold, and brown streaks sprinkled through with strands of blond light enough to be called flaxen was worse than unusual. She'd asked her mother to smooth out the wild colors with a dye that would make her less noticeable, but her mom insisted that ten-year-old kids did not dye their hair.

"I know how you feel though," admitted her mother. "Now I color my hair to cover the gray. Premature gray," she added hastily.

Marley had no idea what age had to do with unsightly hair color, but arguing with her mother was a lost cause.

Now Marley was stuck deciding what to do about Dora.

"Ma'am, er, Dora, are you sure I can't get something for you?" Marley needed help if Dora, who was very pale, fainted.

"I'm all right." Dora cleared her throat. "The birthday card," she said changing the subject, "Who's it for?"

"My mom, Louise Davis. She's thirty-five this week. She doesn't like cards about old age." She bit her lip. Dora was certainly old. Maybe she didn't like to be reminded about it either.

"Well, thirty-five certainly isn't old. That would be my niece's age."

Dora was looking better. Maybe Marley could slip away and buy her card. But Dora was opening her wallet.

Oh, no thought Marley. I hope she won't offer to pay me just for being nice. That would be so embarrassing.

Instead, Dora said, "This is her. This picture was made just before her second birthday."

Marley peered at the photo of a little girl posed on a small red chair. Smiling at the camera she looked excited and sassy.

"Cute," said Marley absently. The toddler was cute, but Marley was more interested in the child's hair. She suddenly saw what had shocked Dora. That hair color was as crazy as her own.

Seeing the picture made Marley uncomfortable. "So, that was the year she passed away?"

"Passed? No, not that we ever knew. She was kidnapped. Stolen from my backyard in Zimmerton." Tears filled Dora's eyes. "Theresa loved playing outside. I'd fenced a space for her and watched from my kitchen window."

Dora drew a tissue from her purse. "I glanced away for only a second. When I looked back, she was gone. The fence had no gate and we never figured out how the kidnapper got inside."

"Theresa," repeated Marley. A name made the child much more real.

Dora stood. "I've taken enough of your time, dear. Don't worry about me." With a sigh, she patted Marley's shoulder and left the store.

Marley's mom was making dinner when she got home. "Hi, honey. Would you set the table?"

As she worked, Marley asked, "Did you have hair like mine when you were my age?"

"Marley, I don't want another argument about coloring your hair. It's beautiful. Besides, chances are good it will change as you get older. Mine did."

"So, your hair was a bunch of different colors, too? But in your grade school pictures, your hair was brown."

Her mother sighed. "It was a dull, muddy brown because your grandmother colored it. I swear it grew so fast that she dyed it every three months. For some reason she hated my real color. Said it looked bizarre. That's one reason I refuse to color yours. You're lovely, not bizarre."

Marley took a deep breath. "Mom," she blurted, "are you adopted?"

Turning from the stove, her mother snickered, "Of course not. My birth certificate is in the lockbox along with Dad's and yours. What's with these off-the-wall questions?"

"No reason. The table's set. Could I . . . ?"

"Go ahead. I'll call you when dinner's ready."

Marley was breathing hard when she pushed the stool in front of the cabinet that stored family photo albums. Although she could barely reach the top shelf, she managed to pull down an album her grandmother, Molly Evans, had made. Leafing through its pages, she found her mom's photos, but none were of her mother before her toddler years. The earliest one showed a Christmas scene with Mom opening a gift. The familiar-looking child, sassy in red pjs, laughed at the camera. Her bedhead hair flared in wildly messy spikes of red, gold, brown, and streaks so bright they could be called flaxen.

Dora said she had lived in Zimmerton, a small town about fifty miles away. There was a mystery to be solved and it scratched at Marley's mind like a fingernail at a mosquito bite. She was certain there was a connection between her mother and the missing Theresa. If Mom had seen the picture Dora carried, she'd be certain, too. Marley knew she'd never be able to let the matter rest. Maybe she could convince her mother to visit Zimmerton and ask some questions. That was the moment Marley began to hatch her plan.

* * *

FIFTEEN YEARS LATER, Marley strode angrily to her battered 2015 RAV4. Just as she threw her bulging backpack into the car's boot, her mother stormed out of the home the family had purchased when Marley was three.

"I'm not asking, Marley. This time I'm demanding that you give up this ridiculous scheme."

Deflating like a missile-shot weather balloon Marley sighed. "This isn't just about you, Mom. We've been over and over this ground. It's time. No, past time."

"I am NOT adopted!" Louise scream-hissed the words as she glanced around to make sure neighbors couldn't overhear. "My birth certificate is genuine."

Marley said nothing. She was certain that her mother was right. Louise Evans Davis was not legally adopted. But Marley was also convinced that her birth certificate, recording a home birth, was as phony as leprechaun gold.

Marley tried one more time. "We need to know . . ."

"We already know what we need to know. It's that woman. That blasted woman, Dora, whoever she is, who put this brain worm in your head."

"Look, I'll only be gone a couple of days. Zimmerton isn't on the other side of the country. And I'm not going to walk around with a banner that cries out 'Look at me, the daughter of the child who was kidnapped right from under your noses fifty-one years ago!'"

Marley didn't bother questioning again why her mother was so dead set against a foray into the small town whose community guide described it as an idyllic place to live. She knew. Louise wasn't convinced that Marley would find nothing. She feared just the opposite.

Hugging her mom, Marley slid into her car and began her journey to uncover the past and influence her future.

The Welcome to Zimmerton sign, announcing Lucious McCallister as mayor, had been newly painted, and evidence of a springtime spruce-up was everywhere. Slowly Marley drove along Main Street past a well-cared-for town square that sported a lovely, huge gazebo and, what looked like, an antique carousel. Just as she spotted Martha's Place, her stomach rumbled, and she decided to chow down before heading to The Daily Zimmertonian to start her research.

Martha turned out to be a real person. She had a day-job as art teacher at Zimmerton High School but continued her family's legacy in food service where she offered the best strawberry pie west of the Ohio River. No lie about that thought Marley as she sampled the dessert.

"The Zimmertonian is right around the corner, honey. The newspaper office is open until five. But you'd be better off researching information at the library. They just digitized their records, and they don't close until eight."

Martha was right. The librarian, Marian Johnson, proudly claiming to be a direct descendant of John Zimmer, escorted her to a computer that held the town's history. Marley was impressed that past issues of the Zimmertonian were also stored and easily accessed.

A few keystrokes later, she found the 1972 article covering the kidnapping of eighteen-month-old Theresa Babic. It related the event as Dora had described it to her. There were no witnesses. No strangers had been noticed in the area. The family members had been absolved of any foul play.

Curious, Marley focused on the family. Theresa had been Cleo and Richard Babic's only child. Cleo's sister, Dora Matthews, had indeed been babysitting the little girl when she'd been stolen. Jon and Anna Matthews, Cleo's parents had been visiting friends in New York and flew home immediately when they learned of the tragedy. So many unfamiliar names thought Marley. How could she meet those people, possibly her people?

She continued searching the 1972 issues and, as she scrolled along, her eye was caught by announcements. A dance at the gazebo, a lavish wedding at the town square, extensive repairs on the town carousel performed by Evans Engineering, and clothing sales from Bob's Men's Store. Soon a related article from 1982 popped up. The piece merely reported that the kidnapping was still unsolved and urged anyone with information relating to the crime to contact the FBI or local authorities. After that, no more information was printed in the Zimmertonian, and the case appeared to have gone cold. Marley copied the newspaper articles and stored them in her backpack.

"Find what you wanted, dear?" asked Marian on Marley's way out.

"Thank you. Yes." But not what I needed Marley thought.

She was considering going back to Martha's for dinner when she passed the town square. Children were waving and calling out as they rotated on the carousel. Something about the carousel nagged at her but she couldn't figure out what. "It'll come, or it won't," she said aloud.

When she entered Martha's, she saw that a line had formed. As she waited to be seated, Martha greeted her. "I have a seat at the counter if you're okay with that," she offered.

"Perfect."

Martha bustled behind the counter as Marley finished her

meal. "That carousel is really a big hit with the kids," Marley remarked.

"I don't know that the downtown would survive as well without it," Martha replied. "We almost lost it a while back. It was aging and, when it broke down in 1972, the town figured it was a goner. The mayor called a friend from out of town to take it for salvage. As I understand, the friend was an engineer who figured he could fix it. He must have done a terrific job. You can see how well it turns and cranks out music."

Marley squirmed on her stool. "The friend who repaired the carousel . . . uh. Well, I saw that his name is Evans."

"Yes, that's right. I believe it's on the plaque in front. Nothing I would know personally, of course. I was born about five years later. But, really, talk about a gift. As I understand, the man would take nothing for the labor or the materials. He took nothing."

Marley felt queasy because she was sure that he had indeed taken something.

* * *

MARLEY SAW NO POINT in waiting to travel home the next day, so she said, "good-bye" to Martha, slid into her RAV4, and headed toward one last stop before leaving town. Richard and Cleo Babic's house drew her like a magnet. By that time Marley was certain that, if she should see the couple, she'd be looking at her biological grandparents.

The house was cheerfully lit, and a woman who must have been Cleo Babic sat reading on the front porch. Marley pulled to the curb for a better look. Soon a man approached the car. He wore a faded sweatshirt and carried a bag of bird seed in one hand and grass clippers in the other.

"Evening, young lady. Saw you sitting at the curb and wondered if you might be lost."

Marley looked at the pleasant-faced man and teared up.

She cleared her throat. "No, sir," she murmured. "I just got something in my eye and pulled over to wipe it."

"Good idea," he said kindly but there was a question in his tone.

Marley caught his piercing stare and self-consciously touched her bright, variegated hair. As much as she wanted to stay, to be invited onto that lovely front porch, to form a connection, she knew she had to leave immediately.

"Drive safely," said the man. "Um," he began.

Marley couldn't risk his asking another question. She certainly couldn't risk his scrutiny. "Thanks," she blurted as she stepped on the accelerator. Looking back, she saw him lingering on the curb staring after her.

It was nearing midnight when she arrived home and discovered her mother still awake.

Like a fretful child, Louise said, "Tell me about your trip to Zimmerton. Did you learn anything? Did you find out what you wanted to know?"

Marley had prepared for this moment during her drive along the dark highway. She was ready with her response. "You can relax, Mom. I didn't find a thing to connect us to the town or the people there. You were right. I spun a fiction from my overactive imagination."

Louise did visibly relax. "Of course," she said brightly. "We know who we are."

"Yes," whispered Marley. "Now we know who we are."

Neighbors

Betsy Taylor

"WHAT DO YOU THINK IS GOING ON?"

"Going on?" echoed Cleo Babic absently, her eyes on her phone.

Richard nodded toward the house next door. "The neighbors."

"What about them?" Cleo's attention shifted at her husband's tone.

"I don't know." He drew his words out thoughtfully. "They seem . . . suspicious."

Cleo, now alert, said, "Suspicious? How?"

"Can't put my finger on it." Richard continued to stare out the window. He stroked the side of his coffee mug.

Cleo relaxed. "They've just moved in. Are still moving in, come to that. We'll meet them when they've settled a bit."

"It's the furniture, I reckon."

"What's wrong with the furniture?" Cleo got up from the sofa and joined Richard at the window.

"There isn't any. Just boxes and a couple of crates."

"Um, that might be odd except that furniture is probably coming along in a moving van."

"A U-Haul arrived yesterday. It was unloaded before lunch." Richard arched his brows knowingly. "Not a stick of furniture." Narrowing his eyes, he went on. "Know what I'm thinking?"

"No, but you'll tell me." Cleo was used to Richard's off-the-wall speculations.

"Remember those news stories about the nice houses that were rented in that Colorado suburb?"

"Colorado?"

"Or Wyoming. Maybe it was Utah. Doesn't matter. Anyway, we saw it on one of the national news programs. Drug dealers rented the properties and installed meth labs and pot farms. Remember?"

"Well, yes. The electric company noticed the unusual amount of electricity being pulled and investigated."

"Right. Right. The raid on one of the houses was filmed. When they went inside, police and DEA officers found the house to have been gutted to make room for processing. The walls were steeped in meth and there was mold everywhere because of the humidity, from the water needed to grow pot."

"So, you think that because you've seen no furniture delivered that . . . ?" Cleo held out her hands palms up in a fait accompli gesture.

"No. Maybe. Well, could be. Those neighborhoods had to be evacuated because some meth labs explode. Just sayin'."

"Richard, darling, retirement doesn't agree with you."

He fell silent. Richard knew she was teasing, but there is truth in jest, as they say.

"You're right. Probably nothing," he conceded.

"Well, let's not make too much of this. After all, this is small-town Zimmerton, not big-city Las Vegas." She gave his arm a gentle pat then chuckled, "Curiosity killed the cat."

"But satisfaction brought him back to life."

Returning to her seat Cleo snickered indulgently. Richard always had to have the last word.

Three days later, coffee mug in hand, Richard returned to his post at the window. Cleo finished clearing the breakfast dishes and ambled toward the bathroom. "After my shower, I'm going to the Horizon Cell Phone Store."

"Why?" mumbled Richard.

"I need an upgrade," she called as she headed down the hallway. Cleo stopped, turned, and reminded him, "So do you. Come with me? We could have lunch at Martha's Place after."

"Have you ever seen our new neighbors?"

"What? Seen them? I guess not. What are you thinking?"

"I think it's very strange."

"Rich – ard. Let it go. So long as they don't throw wild parties that require law enforcement intervention, we'll get along fine. When I asked what you think, I meant about coming with me to the cell phone store."

"Oh, yeah. Maybe." He sounded preoccupied.

Cleo threw up her hands and went toward the bathroom.

"The garage is empty. Has been for a couple of days."

Cleo gave up being irritated and became alarmed. "Richard, what's gotten into you? You sound like a stalker who's been peeping into windows."

"I can see right into the garage with no peeking involved," he barked. "Excuse me for being concerned about the safety of my neighborhood when shady characters invade the block."

"Shady? Augh!! Wanna spy on the house next door? Knock yourself out!" She turned on her heel, her bathrobe swirling like a cape around her as she retreated in indignation.

"Not stalking," grumbled Richard petulantly as he set down his mug. "I'll just go out and add some seed to the bird feeder."

Cleo barely heard the kitchen door close as she turned on the shower faucet.

Half an hour later she emerged from the bedroom dressed and ready to deal with selecting a new phone. "I just want a reliable phone that can let me talk, text, and shoot a few photos," she said aloud. Since Cleo still used maps, she proudly told herself that she didn't even need navigation assistance.

"I'm leaving," she called to the house in general. "Are you coming?"

Richard's jacket was missing from its peg beside the garage door. "Richard?"

Suddenly the house seemed disturbingly empty. The sound of her voice echoed hollowly. Cleo stepped into the garage. His car was there. The door was down. Back in the kitchen, she noticed his coffee mug on the table. Looking out the window she saw a bag of thistle seed on the picnic table. It was expensive but Richard's birds rewarded its purchase by flocking in for a daily show.

Cleo opened the back door and scanned the deck, the patio, and the yard. She called his name.

Like the rest of the properties on the street, theirs extended to a wooded area about a hundred yards behind the house. The privacy was a selling point when the couple had bought the home. But today, empty yards, lack of traffic noise, and lowering clouds created an ominous atmosphere. Although the weather report predicted a cloudy, breezy day, the air was calm as if the Earth held its breath.

Clearing her throat, she scolded herself for her attack of nerves. "All this drama for nothing," she muttered and resolutely strode around the house. Pacing the perimeter revealed nothing. In the end, she found herself standing between her own home and the one next door. The place couldn't have felt more deserted. Could her inquisitive husband have turned housebreaker? Was he even now inside poking around?

She spotted the overturned bucket and realized it had served as Richard's stool over the privacy fence. Following suit, Cleo threw her leg over the barrier and slid down the other side. Now I'm a trespasser she thought.

Cleo's heart nearly stopped when a voice hissed from the murk. "What are you doing here?"

He emerged and Cleo gasped, "Richard, what the heck!"

"Hush."

Cleo wanted to scream. She wanted to throttle him. Instead, she grabbed his arm and pulled. "Let's get out of here," she growled.

"That hole in the foundation wasn't there yesterday. Someone's here," Richard hissed again.

"All the more reason to . . ."

Richard had slipped from her grasp and slid through a gap in the house's foundation.

Cleo glanced around and, against all reason, followed. She found herself in a cellar, hardly more than a crawlspace. The tomblike space pressed in, squeezing the breath from her lungs.

Richard heard her whimper and, remembering her claustrophobia, put his arm around her shoulders.

"Come on, Richard. I heard something. It must be rats." Cleo frantically tugged his arm.

Richard appeared hypnotized, and, before Cleo could budge him, the far wall of the cellar began to glow. Shadows writhed and shimmered in the light as two ghostly figures emerged from a second narrow gash in the foundation. One of them sneezed. The other gasped when he noticed Richard and Cleo.

"Uh," he stammered. Bemused, he lifted his lantern. "Uh, don't be alarmed. We're with the government."

Cloe's heart leapt in her chest as she clutched Richard's jacket.

Befuddled, the two men looked at each other for a moment before recovering. "Here ya go, lady." One of them offered a quick glimpse of a shiny badge before hastily stuffing it back into his pocket.

"Um, yeah. Sorry to scare you," said the other one shaking off his own surprise. "But, uh," he said sharpening his tone, "what are you doing here?"

"Right," accused his partner. "You can't be here. This is private property."

Richard, clearly intimidated, took a step back drawing Cleo with him. "We were curious about . . . about our new neighbors and –."

Cleo, emerging from shock said, "Government? What government?"

One of the men snickered. "*Our* government, lady."

Cleo cleared her throat. "I mean –"

The other man took over. "We're with the Bureau of Land Management."

"Yeah," added the other one. "Like, you know – the Department of the Inferior," he added importantly.

"Cultural stuff." The first man waved his hand in dismissal.

Releasing Richard's jacket, Cleo took a step toward the men. "What cultural 'stuff'?"

The men looked at each other as if deciding what to reveal.

"This is an underground railroad thing."

Suddenly interested, Richard perked up. "Really? Here?" he gazed around the cellar at the dirt floor and crumbly sandstone-block foundation.

"So, we really need you to leave 'cause we're, like, studying the place. The site."

"Understood," said Richard hastily. He was suddenly beset by a creepy feeling prickling along the back of his neck. Pulling Cleo out of the cellar, he noticed that goose flesh had risen along her cheeks.

"This is a classified operation!" One of the men shouted after them.

"Won't say a word," Richard called in return.

"Department of the *Inferior!*" Cleo choked on the word.

"Yeah. Let's make a call."

Behind them the couple heard the men dragging something heavy through the gravelly dirt.

"I have to see," hissed Richard.

"One of those men had a gun tucked under his jacket. This is probably a crime scene. If you go back in there it might become *our* crime scene. Please, Richard. Don't!"

"Watch it!" warned one of the men. Cleo and Richard could hear the urgency in his voice.

"This thing is heavy. Don't just stand there. Help me get it through the tunnel."

"I'm nervy about those two neighbors. We shouldn't have let them leave."

"We'll take care of them soon enough. This chest comes first."

"Right. I can't wait to get out of this creepy hole."

"Are you scared?" his companion taunted. "Think the ghosts of the slaves will git ya?"

"Shut up and pull."

"The chest isn't gonna fit. We shoulda took more time to make the tunnel wider."

"Time." His companion grunted. "We didn't have time. Just push."

Richard couldn't resist a closer listen. He'd just stepped a foot back into the cellar when the whole structure collapsed in a torrent of dirt and stone.

Jumping back, he emerged blinking and spitting grit.

Cleo's initial concern passed as soon as she saw her husband wiping his face and sneezing out dust. "The police are on their way. They're mobilizing the fire department now. I think they're also bringing Mayor McCallister."

Richard coughed. "D-didn't I warn you they were shady characters?"

* * *

THE FOLLOWING WEEK, when the mayor held a press conference, Zimmerton had gone all-out to accommodate reporters from three local Columbus stations as well as those from national networks. Some stations reported humorously that the club of History's Dumbest Criminals had welcomed two new members. Others took the story more seriously describing the potential heist of a chest of Confederate gold.

"Is it really Confederate gold, mayor?" asked a perky reporter. "And how much money would that be?"

"The FBI has taken the chest to scientists for analysis. We've been promised a full report."

"I'll bet," scoffed a voice from the crowd.

Cloe privately agreed that no information would ever be shared with Zimmerton's citizens.

"Where are the thieves?" inquired another reporter.

"One is recuperating at Riverside Hospital in Columbus. The other has been taken into custody. Both are lucky to be alive. When that make-shift tunnel collapsed, the whole back of the house above came down on them. They owe their survival to Cleo Babic who called 911 immediately and to our stellar Zimmerton Volunteer Fire Department for rapidly digging them out."

After Mayor McCallister had finished the press conference, reporters took advantage of Zimmerton's hospitality. Martha's Place sold out of strawberry pie within twenty minutes. The perky young reporter from Columbus rode the carousel while her videographer recorded her joyous spin, and Richard Babic consented to a short interview.

When the excitement died down, the Babics strolled home. "Zimmerton is certainly the focus of a lot of attention today," mused Richard.

"Yes," sighed Cleo thinking about another, more personal, theft. "I wonder. Would we be playing with grandchildren today if attention like this had been paid 51 years ago when our little Theresa was stolen?"

Sally Stops at Stan's Station
Mark Cooper

ANNOYED, SALLY JOHNSON GROANED, "I took my card out too soon!" Such a simple thing, using her credit card at the gas pump. The screen had only two instructions to follow, "Please insert card and wait." But she had pulled the card out before the message on the pump's screen told her to. Now the screen was flashing the message, "Please see cashier to proceed."

She was too busy for this nonsense. Why couldn't a gas pump just read and authorize her card, why this stupid "Please insert and wait" process? In this day and age of instant communication, this was absolutely ridiculous. Why didn't Stanley Shepard, the owner of Stan's Station, have better equipment for serving his customers? Surely the gas station made enough money that he could afford to upgrade to a faster credit card processing system. Come to think of it, why didn't he have more pump islands? It seemed like every time she stopped here for gas, she had to wait in a line before being able to pull up to a pump.

By now Sally was in full steam, I'll bet Stan's a cheapskate, always looking for ways to make a buck. And just look at that truck of his. It's newer than my husband's. That's not fair, my husband works hard to provide for us, he deserves a new truck. Stan probably doesn't care about HIS family. He probably spends all his money on himself. I oughta just buy one of those new electric cars, so I didn't need to buy gas here!

But here she was, stuck. Thankfully Stan's Station did serve good coffee. She certainly needed caffeine to deal with all the frustration she was feeling.

Sally stormed inside. She poured her coffee, a large, and

stirred in one cream and two sugars. Who would believe the price of coffee these days! Almost $2.00 a cup. At a gas station of all places. It isn't like this is an actual coffee shop.

As usual, there was a line at the counter. MORE waiting and MORE delay. She joined the queue. Young Petie Erickson, once a little rascal but now an awkward teenager, was at the counter. "Ah, Mr. Shepard, um, I'm selling raffle tickets for my baseball team. You probably don't want to buy any do you?" Sally had to smile at the boy's hesitancy. Stan gave Petie a big grin. "I think I can do that. How about if I get, oh let's see, maybe $20.00 worth?"

"Really?! Wow, thanks Mr. Shepard!"

The next customer stepped up. "Hi there, Mike!" Stan greeted the young man. "When's that new baby due?"

"Next month. Jody is so excited. And man, I'm kinda scared."

"Ah don't worry too much son. You're a good man. A hard worker. You really love your wife, and she's told me how much you help her. You'll be a good dad, just like you're a good husband."

That's really nice of Stan to encourage that guy so much, Sally thought. She remembered when she and her husband had their first child. They'd lived in the big city back then and knew no one. I wish he'd had someone reassure him like this.

Next, Mrs. Ima Strange stepped up. Her name fit her; she was known for her sharp tongue. "Mr. Shepard, I've told you and told you that your gas pumps are out-of-date and do not function correctly! Every time I try to use my card out there, it doesn't work. I can't imagine why anybody even comes here. This place is a disgrace to Zimmerton!!!"

Sally felt shocked. How could anyone speak so harshly to Stan. She also felt chagrined that she'd had similar thoughts minutes before. But Stan was calming responding to Mrs. Strange. "I'm sorry it's causing you trouble again Ima. You can prepay your gas and you'll be all set."

"Humph!" the unpleasant woman snapped. "I'd might as well get potato chips since I'm already here, even though your prices are highway robbery. I could get these much cheaper in the city!" She grabbed a bag of chips and thrust them at Sam so he could finish her transaction. She then sailed out the door, her nose in the air, the perfect picture of a woman old-timers called a high-flutin' society lady. "See you soon Ima," Stan called after her.

"And how are you today, Sally?"

Sally stepped up to the counter, surprised that Stan remembered her name.

"Hi Stan. I did it again and pulled my card out of the pump's card reader too quickly. Can I prepay $40? And I've got this coffee as well."

"Of course, Sally. You know, most people blame the pumps or me, instead of admitting they might have made a mistake themselves."

Sally felt a pang in her heart. "Oh, at first, I was thinking some nasty things about your pumps. But then I came in and was reminded of how kind and patient you are with everyone. I decided I wasn't going to blame you since it really was my fault. How do you put up with complainers all day?"

"Most customers are nice. As for the rest, I remind myself everyone has problems. And sometimes being rude to others is their relief valve."

"Yes, but what about Mrs. Strange? She was just mean!"

Stan grinned. "Well, despite all her complaining, she is a regular customer. I'll admit that she does get to me now and then. And today I kind of over-reacted."

"You did? I didn't notice anything."

"You saw she got potato chips? She might get home and find them a little bit… crushed. For some reason I 'accidentally' squeezed the bag when I scanned the price."

"Oh Stan!" Sally giggled, "You awful, awful man. Well, I'd better pay and get on my way."

"You got it," Stan answered. "That'll be $40.00."

"You forgot to put my coffee on there."

"Ah Sally, you cheered me up. Coffee's on the house today. See you next time."

"You bet Stan." Sally flashed her smile at him as she turned and left the station. What a nice and generous man and what a nice store!

* * *

AND JUST WHEN YOU THOUGHT it was lost: the missing ingredient from Martha's strawberry pie recipe...

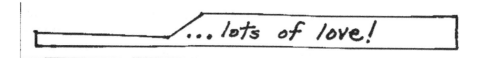

Happy 100th Birthday

Beverly Wencek Kerr

FRANK BYERS STILL LIVED ON the family farm at the edge of town. Born in 1923, he had seen a lot of changes in Zimmerton over the years. Frank was born on that farm and lived there his entire life. For him, it was a happy place and he never wished to leave.

As he sat in his rocking chair on the front porch, he thought back over the years at all the special moments he had encountered in that small town.

Those days as a child were full of fun as Frank and his two sisters, Bonnie and Virginia, would pile into the horse-drawn wagon to go to the Mercantile to get groceries and supplies. They always stopped at Martha's to get a treat of a scoop of ice cream.

How times had changed. Today he has a pick-up truck that takes him wherever he wants to go and uses expensive gasoline for fuel instead of the grass and grain the horses ate. He smiles as he thinks about the fact that you can still go to Martha's for a treat. Now her granddaughter runs the restaurant and strawberry pie is a favorite there.

Those were good days at Zimmerton High School, where he graduated in 1941. He wanted to serve his country during WWII, so it wasn't long before he headed off to Britain as a mechanic in the war effort. Having grown up on the farm, he was used to fixing machines, so it seemed a natural place for him to help. Fortunately, he survived the war. His only thoughts while there were, If I ever return to Zimmerton, I'm never going to leave. It's so peaceful there!

Frank remembered coming back to work on the farm with his

father after the war. They had Holstein cows so morning and evening milking were daily chores that could never be missed. He smiled as he thought about how he changed in 1980 to raising beef cattle that grazed in the summer and ate hay in the winter.

He noticed in the 50s that too many of the young people were leaving the farm for jobs in the city. That was when he decided to begin teaching agriculture at the high school. He made so many friends there over the years from teachers to students. They still drop by for a visit when he is out in his rocking chair on the porch.

Frank was a busy man and had many lady friends over the years but never got married. "I never had time for marriage," he told his friends, "I was always busy with teaching and the farm." Perhaps being a bachelor is part of the reason he lived so long.

The women of the town admired Frank. He was still handsome at 100 years old. They often brought him dinners of roast beef or lasagna and the tastiest sweet treats. There was no pie that he didn't like. The ladies were always proud when he invited them to a dance or a movie. Going out with Frank was a special time.

"Hi, Mr. Byers!" shouted Gavin, a former student, as he pulled up in the driveway. "Good to see you out enjoying the morning sunshine today. I hear it's your 100th birthday. Happy Birthday, Mr. Byers."

"Just another day in paradise for me," answered Frank. "The years come and go pretty quickly. Happy to still be enjoying life on the farm."

"What improvements in farm life have impressed you the most?"

"I'll tell you, the new modern machinery really makes life much easier. I remember Dad driving the horse as it pulled a hay bar mower. When the hay dried, it was raked into piles so it could be moved to store in the barn. You had to be sure the hay was very dry or it would get hot and cause spontaneous combustion and the barn would be lost."

"Today we are lucky to have tractors with cutting bars to cut the fields, then balers to put the hay into nice round or square bales for easy storage. Often people even stack them outside now – sometimes with a tarp over them. I think that is a big improvement."

Soon a car pulled into the driveway. It was Mrs. Zimmer, who was teaching at the high school now. She always dropped by with cookies or cupcakes for Frank to enjoy.

"Happy Birthday, Frank! How's it feel to be 100?"

"Feels great. Glad I was able to see the changes in the world for 100 years."

"What changes have you noticed in our schools?" questioned Mrs. Zimmer.

"When I was teaching thirty years ago, school was a place to learn but also a place to have fun. That seems to have changed these days with all the government regulations and testing that goes on. I always wanted my students to enjoy being at school."

Soon more cars were pulling in the driveway. "Looks like a lot of people are wanting to wish you a Happy Birthday," Gavin announced.

It seemed that everyone in Zimmerton had driven out to the farm for Frank's birthday. Since he had been around for a long time, everyone knew him and wanted to express their appreciation for something he had done for them.

Unfortunately, Frank was the only member of his family who was still left. His parents had died long ago and left the farm to Frank as they knew how much he loved farming. Virginia had been in a fatal accident at an early age so never got to enjoy the small-town life. Sister Bonnie had enjoyed her dream of travel after winning the lottery and he received a message from friends that she had passed away ten years ago at the age of 92 in sunny Florida.

When Bonnie won the lottery, she gave Frank half of her winnings so he would never have to worry about finances as

Happy 100th Birthday

farming income is not always a sure thing. However, Frank lived very reasonably and most of that money was still in the bank invested in a very safe way. Today he was going to surprise everyone.

Everyone brought something to eat as they gathered around Frank on his porch. It was going to be a birthday to remember. Soon Melissa from the bakery enlisted four men to carry the largest birthday cake you could imagine with the number 100 all lit up on the very top of it. There would be a piece for everyone.

Soon all his friends burst into song with,

Happy Birthday to you,
Happy Birthday to you,
Happy Birthday friend Frank,
Happy Birthday to you!

Frank got up out of his rocking chair and walked slowly to the edge of the porch. "My dear friends, I have something special to tell you today on my 100th birthday. You all remember when Bonnie won the lottery and left on her gypsy adventure. Well, before she left, she gave me half of her winnings so I would never have to worry about money."

The crowd gasped as Frank never seemed to have extra money. He lived as he always did. No new trucks or farm equipment. No fancy things for the house. This news really surprised them.

"Today," Frank continued, "I want to give all the money I have invested over the years to the community to build a new library to honor the Byers family. Bonnie left me what was left of her winnings as well so hopefully you will be able to put it all to good use. We love this community and hope that it has a bright future."

A round of applause went up through the crowd gathered. They were all in a state of shock. How much money did Frank have?

Frank felt so proud and relieved now that he knew his money was going for a good cause. This birthday was the best ever! Maybe he could live a few more years and see the new building. Happy 100th Birthday, Frank!

The Feud
Samuel D. Besket

RICK DUNCAN AND BOB WEST had been best friends since the first grade. They were inseparable and often called, "two peas in a pod." Tall and lanky, they liked to play practical jokes on each other and their classmates. Their teachers constantly lamented that the boys should put the same effort into studying as they did pulling pranks. At Mass on Sunday, the Sisters often pleaded, "Lord, why can't these boys just be normal?" It was no use, by the time the boys were in high school, their pranks turned more devious.

Zimmerton High School was a small school by today's standards. Its graduating class was one of the highest-rated in the state and the smallest. The last week before their final senior exams, Principal Harper called Rick and Bob into his office.

"Sit," he commanded, pointing toward two chairs in front of his desk. After shuffling some papers, he laid a file folder with "Senior Exams" typed in bold across the top.

"Mr. Duncan, can you tell me what this is?"

Although he was reading upside down, Rick knew what it was. "It looks like the Senior Exam papers. Why?"

"Why indeed," Mr. Harper shot back, "Why were these found in your locker?"

"These were in my locker?" Rick questioned with a shocked look on his face. "I've never seen this folder before. You were in my locker? Only Bob and I have keys."

"I have a master key," Mr. Harper answered sharply. "The question is how did the exam questions get into your locker?"

After a brief pause, Rick turned and looked at Bob with a

disgusted look on his face. "You did this to me? Of all the stupid tricks. You've gone too far this time Bob. I'll never forgive you for this... never. How could you do this to me? We have been friends for years. You're dead to me."

"It wasn't me," Bob argued. "It wasn't me."

"Quiet," Mr. Harper ordered. "Rick, you're suspended for the rest of the year. It will be up to the school board whether you're allowed to graduate. Now, get out of here."

Turning back to Bob, Mr. Harper sat on the edge of his desk and pointed a finger at him. "If I find out you had anything to do with this, I'll suspend you too. Now get."

Bob ran down the stairs looking for Rick who was storming out the front door. It was too late. Rick wouldn't even look at Bob.

A few days later, Bob tried to call Rick, but he wouldn't answer. Even Rick's mother was cool when Bob called her. All she said was, "It's best you let him cool off." But cool off he never did. Thankfully, the school board allowed Rick to graduate, but he wasn't allowed to participate in commencement activities.

Later that summer, Rick enrolled at Ohio State and Bob enlisted in the Air Force. Four years later, Rick returned home with a degree in business administration. Bob returned home with a slight limp and a Purple Heart. Within weeks, both married their high school sweethearts, but neither attended the other's wedding. Around Zimmerton, the rift between the two was officially called, The Great Zimmerton Feud. "Life just isn't normal since these two aren't friends anymore," the locals moaned. Little did anyone know these two former friends' paths would cross later in an unusual situation.

* * *

FATHER HUNTLEY HAD BEEN AN ALL-STATE OFFENSIVE TACKLE at Zimmertom High School. Everyone was surprised when he turned down offers to play college ball and enter the seminary. Now, twenty years later, he looked like he could still suit up and take the field. He also had proven to be a powerful shepherd to his flock, willing to tackle the most difficult challenges with compassion and wisdom.

Father Huntley stared at the two kids sitting across from his desk. "Of all the people who come in here asking to be married, I never thought it would be you two. Do your parents know you have been seeing each other?"

"No," C.J. admitted. "We met in college. I liked Bobby in high school but knew it wouldn't work out. Daddy would kill me if he knew I was dating Bobby."

Bobby just sat there nodding his head in compliance.

"Well, this might be the answer I've been praying for. I've been trying to get your dads together for years and end this silly feud."

"Oh Lord," he said as he leaned back in his chair, "I'm going to need a lot of help on this one. First of all, I have a few tough questions. C.J. are you pregnant?"

C.J. sat up in her chair as her face turned red. "If you think. . ."

"Now sit back," Father Huntley said as he raised his hand. "I had to ask. It always amazes me when I ask that question that the answer is always 'no.'" But seven months later they have a premature eight-pound baby. I'm just trying to see how much time we have. Have you selected a date?"

"Next spring," Bobby answered back.

"Good, I need time to figure this out. I'll be in touch."

Summer turned into fall and all that C.J. and Bobby heard from Father Huntley was, "I'm still working on it." The kids were getting nervous until they got a call late one night.

"I've sent a registered letter to your parents summoning them to a meeting in my office this Friday the thirteenth. I told them attendance was mandatory if they wished to remain members of the parish, receive the sacraments, or participate in any church functions. I warned them, 'If you're thinking of calling the bishop to complain about what I'm telling you, forget it. You probably guessed I called him and let him know what this is about. And he's on board with me!'"

On Friday afternoon the two families sat in Father Huntley's office with sober looks on their faces. He had the chairs spaced six feet apart allowing him to sit in the middle facing the group. C.J. and Bobby sat on the far end afraid to look at each other.

With a stern voice, Father Huntley began. "We'll open with a prayer. As I said in my letter, don't speak unless I ask you. If you were awake in church, you might have heard me speak on forgiveness. Every time I did, I was thinking of you two men. You're good men, but foolish."

"Bob, do you remember a classmate named Rita Sopa?"

"No can't say that I do Father, why?"

"Rick, do you remember her?"

"Well yes, I was having trouble in my Latin Class. She tutored me. I used to flirt with her just to see her face turn red."

Rick's wife shot him a disgusted look before looking out the window.

"No harm, Father. She knew I was just teasing."

"No harm," Father Huntley shot back as he reached for an envelope on his desk. "I want you to read this letter out loud and you will see what your flirtations caused."

As the Priest handed him the letter, Rick opened it and smiled nervously at his wife.

"Dear Father Huntley," he began.

"If you're reading this letter, you know I lost my battle with cancer. I have instructed my attorney to mail this letter to you as my final wish. I did a terrible thing in high school and want to confess. I was tutoring Rick Duncan in our Latin class. He would flirt with me, and I thought he was interested in a relationship. I was sure he would ask me to the senior prom. When he didn't, I was devastated to the point of doing something foolish."

"During afternoon study hall, I did typing for our principal, Mr. Harper. He inadvertently left the final copy of the exam in the pile of papers I was to type. I made a copy and, after starting a rumor that Bob knew what was on the test, I borrowed Mr. Harper's keys and slipped a copy into Rick's locker. Later I left an anonymous note for Mr. Harper about the test, The rest is history. Until this day, I can't believe I did that. I was so afraid of confessing that I didn't do anything. I hope they will find a way to forgive me if only I could forgive myself for what I did."

Rick handed the letter back to Father Huntley. Laying the letter on his desk, he looked up and was greeted by six stunned stares. After a few minutes, Rick and Bob began shaking their heads. Rick spoke first, "I can't believe I let this happen and how I misjudged you Bob, or shall I say judged you. I'm so sorry."

Bob turned to Rick, "I'll take my share of the blame. It made me feel good when people asked me if you had a copy of the exam. I'm sorry that I helped perpetuate the rumor."

"Well," Father Huntley interrupted, "there's enough blame to go around for everyone. But that is water under the bridge. We have another issue to deal with." Looking at Bobby and C.J., he asked them to stand up. "Rick, Bob, you two have been so engrossed in your feud you didn't know your kids have fallen in love. They came to me months ago to help resolve this problem. Unfortunately, it took Rita's death to solve this issue."

Rick looked at C.J. "Is this true?"

"Yes, Daddy it is."

"Have you set a date?"

"Hopefully next summer after we graduate from college. I know that's a way off, but I want our families to get to know each other again. Maybe a few picnics or cook-outs?"

Rick looked at Bob, "I think the kids are smarter than we are. What do you think?"

"Well, smarter than you anyway," Bob shot back. I'm a little heavier on the gray matter than you buddy!"

"You idiot," Rick fired back, shaking his head. "You couldn't tie your shoes in the first grade if it wasn't for me!"

Father Huntley rocked back in his chair, put his hands behind his head, looked heavenward, and whispered, "Thank you, Lord. Things are finally back to normal. Only next time, please don't take so long."

Zimmerton Zeke, the Worst Weather-Predicting Groundhog Ever

Rick Booth

"THAT AIN'T NO WAY TO treat a groundhog. That's what my grandpap always said about it," snorted Zeb Hosfelt, one of Zimmerton's more successful farmers – and also its most peculiar. As if by annual tradition, at 9 a.m. on February 3rd he would show up at the newsroom of the Daily Zimmertonian just like clockwork, complaining that Punxsutawney Phil, the "official" groundhog of Groundhog Day, was an overgrown, pampered, no-talent rodent that wouldn't know a good weather prediction from a hole in the ground – that hole, of course, being the one he lived in. "They manhandle that critter too much, don't let him sleep natural; wake up natural. That groundhog don't know nuthin'. What you ought to write about is my Zimmerton Zeke. You can count on my Zeke 'cause when he's wrong, he's right. And he's always wrong, you know."

It had likewise become another annual tradition to assign a cub reporter to hear Mr. Hosfelt out, yet stand firm on the paper's policy, that no one wants to hear about a groundhog that makes even worse predictions than Punxsutawney Phil, whose furry clairvoyance gets it right only 38% of the time. This year it was recent journalism grad Georgina Berry's turn to deal with the insistent agriculturalist. "Let him down easy," Pops Werner, the managing editor, had advised her. "He still takes the paper, and we don't want to lose another subscriber."

"Mr. Hosfelt, it's a pleasure to meet you. What can I help you with today?" Georgina began, nervously twirling her pen above a pristine legal pad.

"Well, I think you better let folks know that spring is comin' early this year. Best time to dig your sassafras is right now. Don't wait. See, my groundhog Zeke came out of his hole kind of late in the afternoon yesterday, just after the sky started clearin', and I know he seen his shadow. Now that means he thinks winter's gonna last a mite longer, but Zeke gets it wrong purt near every year. That's how come I know spring's about to start. Ought to let folks know about that, don't you think?"

"Perhaps so, Mr. Hosfelt, but I'm new here and not familiar with a lot of things yet, like your groundhog. Can you tell me more about him?" Georgina replied, trying her gentle best to deflect away from promising to write about Zeke.

"Zeke, see, lives under my barn. Dug his hole right under the southwest corner right after they poured the concrete floor. I don't dare park the tractor close to the hole. That floor cracked years ago, I suppose 'cause Zeke dug out the supportin' dirt. He owes me for that, but since he's good for tellin' the weather, I count the two of us pretty much even about the crack in the concrete. Plenty of room to park the tractor elsewhere," Zeb explained.

"So Zeke dug a hole under your barn and cracked the floor," Georgina recited as she took notes. "When did that happen?"

"Oh, about 1910," Zeb replied casually.

"You mean you built the barn over a hundred years ago?!"

"Well, no, that was my great-grandfather built it, but it was my grandpap that figured Zeke out back when he was a kid."

"So that means you have a hundred-year-old groundhog under your barn?" Georgina inquired with a puzzled look and the passing thought that she was glad to have officemates nearby.

"Well, not really. We've probably had 20 Zekes over all those years. Zeke is whatever groundhog lives in that hole. Must be a good burrow down there, gettin' passed down all those generations. Grandpap started watchin' the first Zeke when he was just 10 years old. He loved deer huntin' so most of the year, when it wasn't deer huntin' season, he'd practice stayin' silent and still and alert by just watchin' that hole hour after hour, pretendin' Zeke was a deer. He'd wait and wait and watch until old Zeke popped out. As soon as Zeke stuck his head out, Grandpap would run to the house to tell his ma he just got a deer. But she knew what that meant. One year she saw an article about Punxsutawney Phil makin' those February predictions based off his shadow. When she read it to my grandpap, sure enough, he set himself to watchin' Zeke every year on the second of February, hopin' his groundhog could beat old Phil. Some years he halfway froze himself to death watchin' all day and Zeke never did pop out. That counted as not seein' his shadow, even if the sun was out that day. See, you don't go pullin' the groundhog out of the ground first thing in the mornin'. You have to be patient and wait."

"That sounds like a very cold hobby, Mr. Hosfelt. I take it you took over your grandpa's groundhog watching a long time ago. Is that right?" inquired the reporter, bemused by the old man's tale.

"Well, yes. I watched Grandpap watch that hole under the barn every year. Then the year I turned 10, back in 1965, I asked if I could sit with him and watch, too. I promised to be super quiet. He said it would be OK, and he'd be glad for the company. We'd sit downwind, and he said we could whisper real soft. We talked a lot on those days, but kept our eyes peeled for Zeke the whole time, too. Some days it was awful cold, and he'd tell me to go in the house and warm up once in a while, but then I'd always come back and help watch some more."

"So did your grandpa figure out that Zimmerton Zeke was a good weather predictor like Punxsutawney Phil? He must have, or I can't imagine putting up with all those cold days if he wasn't," conjectured Georgina.

"Well, that's the strange part. Grandpap kept track of Zeke's predictions every year and compared them to Phil's predictions.

By the time he was in his 20s, Grandpap said he was startin' to see a pattern. It looked like Zeke was gettin' the same prediction as Phil about two-thirds of the time, but the other third, he'd get it wrong – or at least different from old Mr. Punxsutawney. He already had about 55 years of records to look at when I started sittin' with him."

"So it sounds like your Zimmerton Zeke was only right two times out of three, then. Is that what you're saying?"

"Well, yes and no. Grandpap was gettin' a little discouraged that Zeke wasn't up to Phil's standard when I started helpin' him do the groundhog vigil in '65. But I wondered if Phil was really always right. Grandpap and I, we did some diggin' through old almanacs and newspaper records about weather and started to see a pattern. Turns out Punxsutawney Phil was no great weather predicter after all. He only predicted right about one year out of every three. But that gave Grandpap some hope. Maybe, since Zeke didn't always agree with Phil, he thought maybe Zeke could have done better than Phil after all. But it turned out he didn't."

"So you're telling me that Zeke doesn't even predict the start of spring as well as Punxsutawney Phil?" asked Georgina.

"Well, yes and no again. It turned out that every time Zeke agreed with Phil, that was a year when Phil got it wrong. So the *really* bad news was that every year that Zeke disagreed with Phil, that was a year Phil got it right! I been watchin' old Zeke for another 60 years, too, now, 42 years since Grandpap passed away, God rest his good soul. And the pattern is rock solid, I tell you. Zeke gets it wrong every single year! But that's good news, too, if you think about it. It's kind of like one of them Star Wars Jedi mind tricks I use where whatever Zeke predicts, I predict the opposite. So even though Zeke is wrong 100% of the time, I am *right* 100% of the time! That's what separates us from the groundhogs, you know – just knowin' when to use our Jedi mind tricks to predict the weather right when fool groundhogs like my

Zimmerton Zeke get it wrong." Zeb leaned back in his chair with a satisfied grin, expecting Georgina to light up with amazement at the intellectual jujitsu he had just expounded upon. "You can call me Obiwan, if you like," Zeb snickered.

"I've never seen Star Wars. What's an Obiwan?" countered Georgina.

Stunned, Zeb's jaw dropped open for a clean 10 seconds, as if to catch passing houseflies. "Oh, you poor young thing! Do they not teach that in school anymore?"

"No," she paused. "But I think it's brilliant that you know to predict exactly the opposite of Zeke. And you're right. That really is what separates us from the groundhogs. So even though Zeke is a terrible predicter, you're an excellent one. Is that the point?"

"Yes, I suppose it is," Zeb mused, imagining himself someday sculpted in marble when recognized as the new Archimedes. Pausing only a few moments in reverie, Zeb continued, "To be honest, though, I have to confess that there's one year we don't have any record for – 1933 – but every single other year, Zeke got it wrong."

"That's pretty amazing, Mr. Hosfelt. Seems like there ought to be a story there somehow. So what went wrong in 1933?"

"Well, those early 1930s were the Depression years, you know. Have you ever seen that Christmas Carol story about Mr. Scrooge and Tiny Tim?" asked Zeb.

"Oh, yes. I've enjoyed rewatching Dickens' A Christmas Carol almost every year. Does that make up for my not knowing Star Wars?" Georgina giggled.

"That 1932 year leading into 1933 had been really hard on the family back before my time, like in that Dickens story. They didn't have enough to eat, and my father, three-year-old Luke Hosfelt, was startin' to waste away like that Tiny Tim. About all the family could afford to eat was soup. Little Luke, my future father, would take his little spoon and try not to spill a single drop of that precious soup at each meal. They so rarely ate meat that Luke didn't even know what to do with the other utensils set before him on the table. That was the year Grandpap made an extraordinary sacrifice to have a merry Christmas dinner for everyone. Actually, Zimmerton Zeke made the greater sacrifice. On Christmas Day, Little Luke beheld an actual chunk of meat on the plate before him. The poor little boy tried to dig at it with his spoon, but to no avail. That's when my Grandpap came to the rescue and told him, 'Use the fork, Luke.'" Zeb erupted in laughter, but Georgina just stared at him, nonplused.

"Was that another Star Wars joke?" Georgina inquired. Zeb continued to snicker while nodding his head 'yes.' "But did they really eat the groundhog that year?"

A serious look came down like a lead curtain over old Zeb's face. "Yes, but it was all for a very good cause. Groundhogs don't change holes in mid-winter, so Grandpap didn't get a Zeke prediction in 1933. Mind you, that was back before he knew Zeke was always wrong. But lookin' back years later, Grandpap and I became convinced that if Zeke had dodged that bullet – literally – he would have been wrong in 1933, too!"

"Mr. Hosfelt, the story you have told me is quite amazing, and I wish I could tell you the Daily Zimmertonian could publish a front page article about your Zeke, but I think the editorial board here has misgivings about touting a furry little critter that does even worse than Punxsutawney Phil. I think that after the novelty wore off, it just wouldn't look good to have the 'world's worst' of anything here. On the other hand, since Zeke is so bad at predicting the weather, he's made you extremely good at it. You know, that Jedi hat trick you mentioned."

"Mind trick," Zeb corrected. "Hat trick is hockey. It's a *mind* trick I use on the groundhog."

"Were there groundhogs in Star Wars, Mr. Hosfelt?" Georgina suddenly wondered.

"Oh, you poor dear! No. It's an Obiwan thing."

"You know, Mr. Hosfelt, I wish I could just write an article about how good you are at predicting the end of winter, but you're not an adorable, furry little animal. People predicting the weather right just doesn't seem newsworthy. Unless they're ghosts. Ghosts or Zombies."

"Would it help if I stopped shaving?"

"Not really. Have you ever seen Bigfoot? If you've seen Bigfoot, I could write about that and mention your great weather predictions in passing. What do you think?"

"Sounds reasonable to me, except I've never seen Bigfoot. You know, my neighbors out in Adams Township always like to hear about Zeke's wrong predictions which I jujitsu into correct ones. Everyone out there in Adams knows right when to dig sassafras," Zeb bragged.

"I'm glad to hear that our local farmers, at least, are getting some good out of your groundhog, so to speak. No more 'using the fork,' though, I hope!" Georgina exclaimed.

"Nope, and I hope we never have to eat Zekeburgers again. I think I understand better now why Zimmerton Zeke just ain't newsworthy. The Daily Zimmertonian is just keepin' up the community standards, I guess. But to let you know, I'm workin' on another critter that I hope will be worthy of a mention in the Zimmertonian someday. She's my parrot. I call her Powerball Polly, but she gets it wrong a lot, too."

"Oh, what does Polly do?" asked Georgina.

"See, I put a fresh Powerball ticket at the bottom of her cage each week and then keep watching it. The first time I see a dropping on a Powerball pick and five of the other numbers, I pull the card and see if she got those numbers right, come the next drawing. She does better than Zeke but still only gets about half the numbers right. My neighbors like to bet what she picks, too."

"Well, that's wonderful, Mr. Hosfelt," said Georgina, trying not to sound condescending. "Thanks so much for coming in.

Maybe next year we can oblige you with an article if your parrot comes up to snuff. Unfortunately, it seems your Zimmerton Zeke is such a loser, we may never be able to write about him in our upbeat hometown publication. Wouldn't fit with the community image. Good luck with your Powerball Polly. When she starts predicting the numbers right every time, we'll finally have something to write about!" Georgina concluded, standing up and offering her hand to Mr. Hosfelt, no longer concerned about needing officemates nearby.

As Zeb Hosfelt walked out of the Daily Zimmertonian office building, he remembered his next errand of the morning. The wad of bills in his wallet was too big for comfort, so he headed for the bank. Though Powerball Polly had never yet hit the grand prize, her droppings were already returning a more modest, but consistent, 50-to-1 on average. If the Daily Zimmertonian didn't think his Zeke was newsworthy or that Polly wasn't precise enough to meet their publication standards, that was just fine with him.

Zeb then smiled. He smiled and began to laugh. Zeb smiled and laughed all the way to the bank.

Made in the USA
Middletown, DE
01 November 2023

41731377R00106